W9-DEZ-010

Endorsements

"Local economic growth requires true leadership. Dr. Gordon's 25 years of experience in Fairfax County have yielded the kinds of valuable insights that can benefit other communities."

Steven L. Davis
Chairman, Fairfax County Economic Development Authority and Former Senior Executive, Exxon Mobil Corporation

"As the Congressman from Virginia's 11th Congressional District, I was aware that the economic growth of the entire Washington, D.C., region, as well as that of the Commonwealth of Virginia, was largely dependent upon what happened in Fairfax County, Virginia."

The Honorable Thomas M. Davis III
Former United States Congressman

"Through a Fulbright grant for Senior Scholars, Dr. Gordon has made invaluable contributions to the economic planning of the North Highlands region of Scotland. His counsel to a community that is about to lose its primary employer and financial resource has been comprehensive, insightful, and motivational."

Lord Robert MacLennan
Member, British House of Lords

"Dr. Gordon has provided a comprehensive, analytic and clear look at the importance and complexity of economic growth. His book provides a necessary framework and concrete examples. He nicely separates facts from opinions, and delineates both the subjective and objective aspects of economic growth. His style makes this an important read for both the expert and the student."

Dr. Alan Merten
President, George Mason University, Fairfax, Virginia

"Dr. Gordon's service as an adjunct professor at the Catholic University of America gives our students an opportunity to hear from an acknowledged expert about how local economies grow and develop. This book will be a valuable addition to the literature in the field because it was written by an accomplished academic and a leader in the economic development profession."

Dr. Phillip Henderson
Chairman, Department of Politics, Catholic University of America,
Washington, D.C.

"Fairfax County and the southeast of England have established a partnership that has been beneficial to both sides of the Atlantic. Fairfax County is in the forefront of international economic development."

Michael Dewick
Head of International Business—Americas, South East England
Development Agency

THE FORMULA FOR ECONOMIC GROWTH ON MAIN STREET AMERICA

American Society for Public Administration
Book Series on Public Administration & Public Policy

Evan M. Berman, Ph.D.
Editor-in-Chief

Mission: Throughout its history, ASPA has sought to be true to its founding principles of promoting scholarship and professionalism within the public service. The ASPA Book Series on Public Administration and Public Policy publishes books that increase national and international interest for public administration and which discuss practical or cutting edge topics in engaging ways of interest to practitioners, policy-makers, and those concerned with bringing scholarship to the practice of public administration.

The Formula for Economic Growth on Main Street America, Gerald L. Gordon

The New Face of Government: How Public Managers Are Forging a New Approach to Governance, David E. McNabb

The Facilitative Leader in City Hall: Reexamining the Scope and Contributions, James H. Svara

American Society for Public Administration
Series in Public Administration and Public Policy

THE FORMULA FOR ECONOMIC GROWTH ON MAIN STREET AMERICA

GERALD L. GORDON

CRC Press
Taylor & Francis Group
Boca Raton London New York

CRC Press is an imprint of the
Taylor & Francis Group, an **informa** business

CRC Press
Taylor & Francis Group
6000 Broken Sound Parkway NW, Suite 300
Boca Raton, FL 33487-2742

© 2010 by Taylor and Francis Group, LLC
CRC Press is an imprint of Taylor & Francis Group, an Informa business

Library of Congress Cataloging-in-Publication Data

Gordon, Gerald L.
    The formula for economic growth on Main Street America / Gerald L. Gordon.
        p. cm. -- (American Society for Public Administration book series on public
        administration & public policy)
    Includes bibliographical references and index.
    ISBN 978-1-4200-9389-6 (hardcover : alk. paper)
    1. Economic development--United States. 2. Community development--United States.
3. Local government--United States. I. Title. II. Series.

    HC110.E44G67 2010
    338.973--dc22   2009022514

Visit the Taylor & Francis Web site at
http://www.taylorandfrancis.com

and the CRC Press Web site at
http://www.crcpress.com

This book is dedicated to my wife and family as well as to the men and women of the staff and commission of the Fairfax County Economic Development Authority. Their collective wisdom, effectiveness, and dedication are constant sources of inspiration.

Contents

List of Figures

List of Tables

Preface

It is not always evident why economic growth takes root in one area over another. Even within a single region, some communities may outpace their neighbors in securing the economic growth that leads to an enhanced quality of life. Although some commonalities in these situations may be identifiable, many communities possess similar assets and implement apparently similar economic development plans, yet have experiences that are vastly different—perhaps even diametrically opposed. Indeed, economic growth in the United States in the late 20th century was marked by the dramatic rise of some communities and the equally stunning demise of others.

There are lessons that can be gleaned from the varied experiences of communities that are replicable elsewhere throughout the United States. There are also factors and policies that can make the application of those lessons more or less likely to succeed in other communities. Examples of communities where public policies and general directions have damaged the local economic base in both the short and long terms abound. The communities that do not shift their strategic focus stand the risk of becoming secondary to the growth markets of tomorrow. They will be the suppliers, shippers, and bedroom communities that exist to support the advancement of others.

The Formula for Economic Growth on Main Street America examines the growth and decline of communities and identifies the key components of sustained economic growth as well as policies and actions (or inactions) that can be precursors to the decline of the local economic base. The case studies, derived largely from direct experience, provide insights that will be instructive for policy makers and practitioners as well as students of public administration. Readers can superimpose the concepts highlighted herein onto real-world examples and examine the following questions being asked today by community leaders:

- What is actually meant by the term "local economic growth," and why would anyone want it in their "own backyard"? What are the benefits and costs of slow, dramatic, or no growth?

- Who have been the winners and losers in terms of economic growth, and why?
- Why does the growth of some communities within a single regional marketplace dramatically outpace that of their neighbors when all seem to possess similar advantages of location, assets, and amenities?
- What lessons have been learned by the case study communities that can be replicated elsewhere, and what circumstances must be in place for those lessons to apply?
- How can smaller or mid-sized communities, or those in rural areas, benefit from these examples and effectively pursue and sustain economic growth?
- What steps can the elected and administrative leadership of communities—large or small, urban or rural, growing or in decline—take to stabilize and enhance the growth of their cities and towns over time?

In recent years, it has become clear to communities that sustained local economic growth can enable the provision of public services for growing populations while minimizing the tax burden for residents. In today's environment, financial institutions that were once believed to be rock-solid have collapsed, and federal intervention in the financial sectors that underlie the well-being of the nation and the world has been exercised as a last resort. Individuals have lost their savings and companies have gone out of business. As companies fail and individuals lose their jobs and their ability to provide for their families, communities suffer. It is generally a time of local reflection upon methods of growing the economy to avoid such devastating impacts in the future.

Communities, in difficult economic times, lose significant tax revenues—income taxes, property taxes, business taxes, and user fees—as the local, regional, national, and global economic foundations crumble. And, as revenues decline, the demand for the public services that are funded by those revenues increases. When the unemployment rate rises, demand for welfare and other human services transfer payment increases. A direct relationship can often be found between rising rates of joblessness and crime. Again, this translates into increased costs for public services at a time when the revenue base is declining. More police, fire services, and support for families in need may be required. At the same time that the local ability to provide the necessary services is declining, the private nonprofit organizations that can often supplement public programs may find their sources of financial support—both public and private—also waning.

Most communities today are experiencing budgetary difficulties. The collective value of housing in the United States has declined. Real estate tax revenues are down. Commercial properties have greater levels of vacancies than in the past, resulting in little demand for new construction. Again, the real estate tax base is adversely affected. Unemployment is on the rise, which means that unemployment compensation costs are rising and income tax bases are eroding. Just as individuals' personal investments are losing value, so are the investments of communities. This creates further pressure on local governments, and they respond with layoffs of their own, employee unpaid furloughs, and draconian budget cuts.

Some community leaders are confronting these conditions today from slightly better positions than others. They are the communities where the local economy was strong prior to the general decline; those economies had higher points of performance from which to decline. Local economies that were already weak—where nonresidential tax revenues were minimal and unemployment rates high—may now find themselves in complete disarray, with no ability to provide for what are now not just constant levels of demand for public services of a wide variety, but increasing levels of demand for public services.

Local economic growth must come to be regarded as *de rigueur* for local governments and their elected leaders. And strong programs to pursue local economic growth must come to be regarded not as costs, but rather as essential investments. These are not partisan issues. Growth enables local elected officials to enhance the quality of life of their constituents. These are not Democrat or Republican issues.

The community that remains relatively strong economically will sustain itself through adverse economic times. Localities that attempt to build an economy from scratch at the bottom of economic cycles will confront a variety of hardships that will affect the community and its residents. Many of the case examples used in this book learned that lesson from difficult economic times and will weather the current storms more effectively because they have adjusted and grown their economies, and have created an environment that is conducive to business growth. That provides a decent quality of life in the good times and sustenance in the bad.

The Formula for Economic Growth on Main Street America examines local economic growth and its many iterations and implications. For communities in growth mode and for those in decline, its lessons can help policy makers chart new courses.

About the Author

Dr. Gerald L. Gordon is the president and chief executive officer of the Economic Development Authority (FCEDA) in Fairfax County, Virginia, one of the largest office space markets in the United States. He has been with the FCEDA for twenty-five years, during which office space in the county grew from 32 million square feet to more than 107 million, the job base grew from 243,000 to more than 600,000, and the real estate tax rate was reduced from $1.47 to $0.92. The FCEDA was named by *Site Selection Magazine* as one of the top ten economic development organizations in North America, and in 2007, *Time* magazine called Fairfax County "one of the great economic success stories of our time."

Dr. Gordon has taught at the University of Maryland, George Mason University, the Catholic University of America, and Virginia Commonwealth University. He has consulted with city and state governments throughout the United States as well as the Republic of Poland, the island of Vieques in Puerto Rico, the Scottish North Highlands, and the Federated States of Micronesia. He has consulted with various federal agencies, associations, businesses, nonprofit organizations, universities, the U.S. Navy, and the United Nations. Dr. Gordon holds a bachelor's degree from The Citadel, a master's degree from George Washington University, and a doctorate from the Catholic University of America. This is his eighth book; his others include topics ranging from strategic planning to economic development. Dr. Gordon is the 2003 recipient of the prestigious Israel Freedom Award and, in 2006, became the first American to address the All-Parliamentary Exports Group in the British House of Commons. Dr. Gordon is a Fulbright senior scholar and a fellow of the International Economic Development Council.

Chapter 1

Defining Economic Growth in a Changing Business Climate

1.1 Introduction

"Local economic growth." The phrase seems universally appealing. Yet, there are many communities today that do not want to pursue the economic growth of their community or, at least, do not wish to pursue further growth. The resultant debates often polarize participants around positions with easy labels: "pro-growth," "no-growth," and "smart growth."

Elements of these debates often become emotional for communities. For some, growth is regarded as essential for survival—that is, in the absence of growth, there can only be decline. It further appears that one person's growth can be another's loss, and smart growth is redefined each time it is used in a different context. In reality, the aspects and impacts of growth are indeed very different from one community to the next, as circumstances change. But, the role that localities can play is a critical one. Henry Cisneros wrote that "America's economy is made up of a diverse mix of local economies."[1] Thus, the economy of this nation is, to a great extent, a composite of the effects of all the decisions made in America's cities and towns about the future of growth in their own economies.

Not only does our understanding of what the term "local economic growth" implies change from one place to the next, it also changes as we regard it over time. What community leaders generations ago saw as growth, along with its attendant benefits and detriments, is no longer the way we regard it today. One can assume from that premise that our comprehension today will differ from the ways in which local economic growth will be regarded in the future. It is therefore critical first to understand what has been meant by local economic growth. Such an understanding can help provide a clearer vision of what the communities will need and how best to pursue it.

1.2 Economic Growth in Post–World War II America

World War II created changes in American life that were born of necessity rather than planning. As the men of the generation who were in their prime working years entered the military and left their communities for service overseas, the jobs at home fell to women and older and younger workers. Women assumed positions in industry, many of which were vital to the war effort, and that had previously been the bastion of male workers.

Over the course of several years, many of the females who had entered the labor force learned that there were things they could do outside of the home to earn a living. Many of them lost their jobs to the returning servicemen at the conclusion of hostilities; some were happy to return to their previous lives as homemakers, but many were not interested in giving up their new-found freedom and earning power. In short, not all women were satisfied to have worked only "for the duration."

Bean and Leach wrote that "the economic prosperity of the post-war years generated greater demand for their services. Thus, women began to enter, or re-enter, the labor force in greater numbers than before."[2] Notwithstanding the implications for the American family and culture, this trend prescribed greater demands for communities to enhance their local economies and to create more jobs than ever before. The emergence of the two-income family meant that cities, towns, counties, and regions needed to create jobs for a larger workforce. The economic boom that followed was, in large measure, both due to and the cause of a redoubled workforce.

To a great extent, then, the post–World War II view of local economic growth had its basis in the increasing demand for employment opportunities. Concurrently, U.S. and global economic expansions meant that there would be new job opportunities to meet the demand.

Individuals and families began to demand more household consumer items, including automobiles, kitchen appliances, and television sets. As the resultant production increased, so did the regions in which the facilities were located. Not only did the current residents help fuel growth, but plants and facilities served to attract new workers from areas where fewer opportunities existed.

Following World War II, troops came home and Americans displayed a desire to raise families. The prior three decades had seen two world wars and the Great

Depression, and Americans wanted to return to normal lives. "For much of this century, but especially since World War II, the American dream has centered on owning a car and a detached house in the suburbs with lawn, garden, and responsive government, good schools, a quick commute to work, and fresh air."[3]

These trends fostered changes in manufacturing, including the ability of the American automobile industry to convert from war production back to the manufacture of passenger vehicles and the growth of affordable housing fueled by the baby boom and the availability of lower-interest mortgages for returning servicemen, in particular. Together, the result was the growth of cities and towns, and a thirst for sustained economic growth around them. Table 1.1 shows the growth of home ownership in the post–World War II United States. Notice the jump between 1940 and 1960.

As the population grew nationwide, cities expanded. New communities were developed and old communities boomed, most notably in the southern tier of the United States. The resulting growth of cities and towns yielded new sets of expectations. As populations grew, there were increased demands being voiced for new schools, roads, parks, public safety, and other public services from the communities that were now home to larger numbers of residents. City councils and county boards began to feel the pressure to levy additional taxes to help pay for the marginal increases in the costs attendant to such growth.

But, America's communities were not all similarly affected. Anthony Downs wrote that, between 1950 and 1996, the metropolitan populations of the Northwest and Midwest "declined from 63 percent of the nation's metropolitan totals to less than 45 percent. During that same period, the proportion of the metropolitan

Table 1.1   U.S. Home Ownership Rates

Year	%
1940	43.6
1950	55.0
1960	61.9
1970	62.9
1980	64.4
1990	64.2
2000	66.2

Source: U.S. Bureau of the Census. "Census of Housing." Washington, D.C.: 2004.

population living in the western and southern United States increased from less than 40 percent to more that 55 percent."[4]

As the population shifts continued through the 1950s and into the 1960s, cities and suburbs grew at the expense of more rural areas. At the same time, technological advances enabled larger farming concerns to produce on a massive scale, which further motivated the nation's small farmers to relocate to areas where manufacturing jobs were available. The U.S. Department of State reported that "farming became a big business ... As a result, the number of people working in the farming sector which, in 1947 stood at 7.9 million, began a continuous decline; by 1998, U.S. farms employed only 3.4 million people."[5] And the rate of growth of America's suburban families outpaced the rate of urban family growth by a ratio of five to one.[6]

Many of the population shifts occurred in the South and Southwest, spurring massive development in and around major cities. The online *Columbia Encyclopedia* reports that, by 1990, Los Angeles, Houston, Dallas, San Diego, San Antonio, and Phoenix were among the ten largest cities in the United States. Further, as these cities grew, the population densities of some of the inner cities increased rather dramatically, as is illustrated in Table 1.2 and graphically in Figure 1.1. Two cities—Dallas and San Antonio—show declines in population densities over that period, while Phoenix's population density remained flat. It should be noted that some of the Sun Belt cities, as they matured during this time frame, also expanded geographically. This, of course, had an effect on the population densities reflected in the table. However, the trends are indicative of the changing needs of these cities as their economies evolved. For sake of comparison, Table 1.3 and Figure 1.2 reflect the same measures in four Rust Belt cities—Detroit, Cleveland, Milwaukee, and Buffalo—over the same period of time. As these are more mature cities, the geographic boundaries did not change substantially over the time frame reflected in the table.

Table 1.2   Sun Belt Population Densities (Per Square Mile)

City	1940	1950	1960	1970	1980	1990
Los Angeles	3,356	4,370	5,451	6,073	6,384	7,427
Houston	5,282	3,726	2,860	2,841	2,867	3,020
Dallas	7,259	3,879	2,425	3,179	2,715	2,941
San Diego	2,134	3,364	2,979	2,199	2,736	3,428
San Antonio	7,111	5,877	3,662	3,555	2,992	2,811
Phoenix	INA	6,247	2,343	2,346	2,437	2,342

Source: U.S. Census Bureau, *Population of the 100 Largest Urban Places,* June 15, 1998.

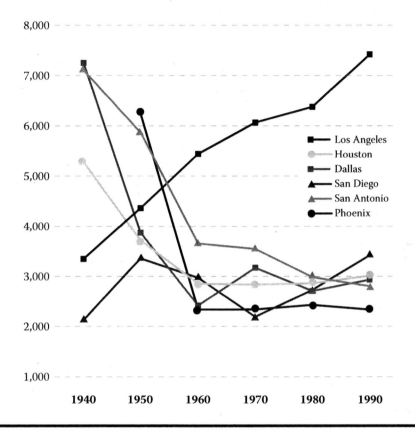

Figure 1.1   Sun Belt population densities (per square mile).

Some observers believe that the economic outlook of the Rust Belt cities may be less bleak in the future. The theory of dynamic equilibrium, as applied to local economic growth, implies that "the infrastructure of a leading region may succumb to aging and obsolescence. Investment in new industries may be more efficient in the lagging region, and may actually leapfrog older generations of technology and techniques, and move directly to the latest and most effective and efficient technologies and practices."

Thus, manufacturing relocation from the Rust Belt to the Sun Belt is explained in part by the greater investment returns available in the South and West relative to tearing down and rebuilding infrastructure in the North. However, regional life-cycle theory suggests that "newly developed regions will themselves decline and…bypassed regions will have been retooled. One should thus expect an eventual decline of the Sun Belt and the re-emergence of the Rust Belt."[7] In reality however, although some changes to the infrastructure of bypassed regions may be advanced, the Rust Belt will never be able to retool its climate to match those with less severe extremes.

Table 1.3   Rust Belt Population Densities (Per Square Mile)

City	1940	1950	1960	1970	1980	1990
Detroit	11,773	13,249	11,964	10,953	8,874	7,411
Cleveland	12,016	12,197	10,789	9,893	7,264	6,566
Milwaukee	13,536	12,748	8,137	7,548	6,641	6,536
Buffalo	14,617	14,724	13,522	11,205	8,561	8,082

Source: U.S. Census Bureau, *Population of the 100 Largest Urban Places,* June 15, 1998.

As the regional economies of the Sun Belt evolved, they had not only the challenges of growth and raising tax revenues for public service provision, but also faced the growth of poverty that resulted from too many people and too few jobs, issues that continued over time. Of the twenty-five metropolitan areas with the lowest per capita income in 1990, twenty-three were in the Sun Belt, according to the online *Columbia Encyclopedia.* As these communities addressed the direct and indirect impacts of this in-migration, the physical structure often grew faster than their capacities to keep pace with infrastructure and planning. "Indeed the most damning indictment against the Sun Belt city is the atrophy of classical urban (and

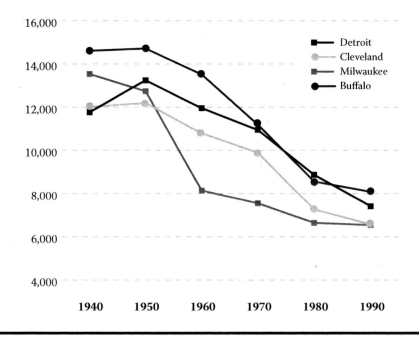

Figure 1.2   Rust Belt population densities (per square mile).

pro-environmental) qualities like residential density, pedestrian scale, mass transit, and a wealth of public landscapes."[8]

The Sun Belt grew as Americans migrated from the industrial areas of the Northeast and Midwest. As manufacturers made the same trek southward and westward, the communities they left lost much of their tax base and were left with lower-income populations in even greater need of public services without the benefit of the business tax base that yielded requirements for relatively fewer services than did residents.

As cities grew, their suburban areas also expanded, creating new communities with new issues to address and a new set of issues and relationships for cities to address. Between 1950 and 2000, U.S. metropolitan areas grew by more than 141 million people.[9] And by 1990, only 28 percent of all U.S. employment remained inside city limits.[10] Major cities suffered from the loss of their higher-income families to the new and more spacious suburbs, and the loss of much of the middle class to the greater region. In these new suburban areas, residents could afford more land and raise their families in a less intense environment. And, as Anthony Downs noted, "cities are not only poorer on average, they also house disproportionate numbers of persons below the poverty level and exhibit higher levels of unemployment and crime."[11] This, in turn, makes the city an increasingly less desirable location for business. Cisneros wrote that "decaying physical and institutional infrastructure, rising crime rates, and the potential for more widespread social unrest associated with poverty make the city an increasingly expensive location."[12]

The businesses that had been located within city borders observed the outflow of the best educated residents to the suburbs and began to follow suit. After all, those were the employees that many growing businesses wanted. As a result, in the decade of the 1990s, 90 percent of all new office space was constructed in suburban locations.[13] This is both a reflection of the exodus of businesses from cities to suburbs and a force that continued to impel the trend.

As the center cities were left increasingly to lower-income individuals, crime rates increased and the exodus to the suburbs accelerated. As jobs were lost, the city's remaining residents required increasing levels of social services at the same time the tax base was dwindling. As Marshall explains, "now the suburb dominates...It is the suburbs that are now the center of commerce, industry, and business...Parts of the city are actually becoming the suburbs to the suburbs."[14] That can certainly be said of the Washington, D.C., region, where more jobs exist in suburban Fairfax County, Virginia, than in the center city, and where that gap is growing greater each year.

New York City, for example, lost nearly one million residents during the decade of the 1970s and narrowly avoided bankruptcy. In fact, Mayor Beame found it necessary to establish a priority for the payment for services to be made: police, fire, sanitation and public health services; food and shelter for people dependent on the city; hospital and emergency medical care for those with no other resources; bills from vendors of essential goods and services; school maintenance; interest on city debt; and payments due the retired and aged. The approach was dubbed by Roberts as "rational and humane" (Nytimes.com, December 31, 2006).

But although New York's approach may have been rational, it belied a situation that was being replicated in other American cities, large and small, old and new. Cities were becoming the domain of those who could not afford to move to the suburbs where the jobs were to be found, where the best schools were located, and where the overall quality of life seemed to be substantially better. Urban America was becoming home to increased crime, lower salaries and expendable incomes, and a variety of challenges for the political leadership. The result was financial disaster. In 1975, Roberts noted, the city of New York asked Manufacturers Hanover, the city's paying agent, "to remain open late to assemble a package of $453 million to pay off short-term debt due that day" (Nytimes.com, December 31, 2006).

Entire regions of the country were also losing both people and jobs. The nation's Rust Belt was the traditional manufacturing region of the United States. Arthur O'Sullivan notes that, as late as 1947, it housed 70 percent of America's manufacturing jobs.[15] Gillham contrasts that with data from three years later (1950), by which time more than half of all industrial employment in the country was found in suburban locations.[16] But between 1960 and 2000, the industrial cities of the Rust Belt and elsewhere lost population in dramatic numbers, as is shown in Table 1.4 and graphically represented in Figure 1.3.

O'Toole notes that, since 1990, all of the forty fastest-growing metropolitan areas in the United States are in the West and South, and thirty of the thirty-five urban areas that lost the greatest percentage of population were in the Northeast and Midwest.[17] In short, cities too often confronted a downward spiral fostered by the very conditions that would make it increasingly difficult to reverse their fortunes.

Table 1.4   Population Losses in Industrial Cities, 1960–2000

City	1960	2000	Percentage Change
Cleveland	876,050	478,403	−44.6
Detroit	1,670,144	951,270	−43.0
Baltimore	939,024	651,154	−30.7
Philadelphia	2,002,512	1,517,550	−24.2
Milwaukee	741,324	596,974	−19.5
Newark	405,220	273,546	−32.5

Source: U.S. Census Bureau, *Statistical Abstract of the United States,* 2003.

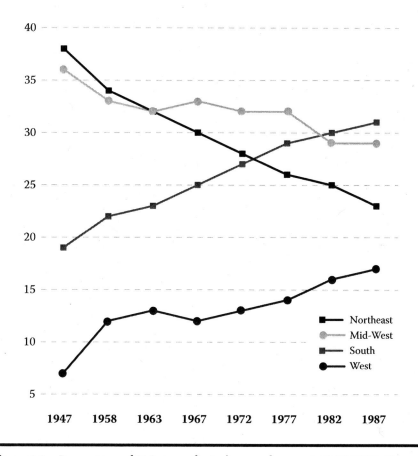

Figure 1.3 Percentage of U.S. manufacturing employment, 1947–1987. (*Source:* U.S. Department of Commerce, 1987 Census of Manufacturing, in Richard D. Bingham and Robert Mier, *Theories of Local Economic Development: Perspectives from Across the Disciplines,* Newbury Park, California: Sage Publishers, 37.)

1.3 Changing Views of Community Economic Growth through the 1970s, 1980s, and 1990s

The 1970s and 1980s witnessed significant national and international economic events, the impacts of which were felt in communities and rural areas throughout the United States. Recessions in 1973 and 1982 were coupled with high levels of inflation as well as unemployment. Interest rates were high enough to dampen spending, and overall economic growth was minimal.

Then, as the 1980s growth began to swell consumer confidence, the 1987 stock market decline quickly dampened enthusiasm for growth. Growth of communications technologies finally began to take hold late in the decade of the 1980s, driving a new spirit of American entrepreneurialism and business start-ups. As will be noted later, however, the economic boom was significantly uneven in its geographic distribution. Not all parts of the country grew at the same rate and some experienced decline even as the general economy expanded. And even parts of regions grew while other parts suffered. Urban, suburban, and exurban areas did not share equally in the growth.

Ultimately, the suburbs would grow and reach their capacity, driving up the cost of land and housing, giving rise to another ring of development even further out from the center cities that would come to be known as "exurbs." Bruegmann defines these areas as being "the very low-density region beyond the regularly built suburbs that is still economically and socially tied back to the central cities."[18] The process of constant movement outward from the original focal point—the city— has become known as "sprawl." This is not really a new phenomenon, as will be discussed later; however, it should be noted that each new outer ring of development creates new demands for the neighboring inner rings.

William Hudnut cites a distinction between what he terms "good sprawl," which generates demand for new housing and service businesses, and "bad sprawl," which leads to congestion, environmental impacts, and various "hidden costs" and inequalities.[19] As the exurbs became the bedroom communities for the suburbs, there were a series of consequences: inner cities lost jobs and their higher-income residents, suburbs have had to create jobs to support their residents and those of the exurbs, exurban communities have incurred the costs of residential growth without the benefit of a business tax base, and the regions have encountered new demands for housing, transportation, and other infrastructure.

The Policom Corporation published a report that stated the number of U.S. metropolitan areas to be 316. Those metro areas account for about 80 percent of the American population, causing a constant push of sprawl further and further outward from the area's center.[20] Over time, the inner rings of regional development have taken on the characteristics of their neighbors even closer in. "Many of the inner suburbs look and feel like the adjacent communities within the central city. The differences between city and suburb have blurred as the suburbs have become more diverse and heterogeneous than ever."[21]

And infrastructure networks are stressed by the growth of outer rings of communities and the similar exodus of employers. "The old edge-to-center commute that once loomed so large has been submerged in a new pattern where there are often more people commuting out from the historical center to jobs in the suburbs than from the suburbs into the center."[22]

Finally, as former Indianapolis Mayor William Hudnut argues, the lower densities at the outer edges of regional growth have created such wide discrepancies between parts of single regions that it is increasingly difficult for regions to establish a true sense of community. By polarizing contiguous communities, the sprawl has consistently resulted in psychological and social costs, as well as infrastructural costs and the loss of environmental resources.[23]

Local economies grew in the late 1990s as new technologies helped lower production costs and generate interest in consumer consumption. As the costs of new technology products dropped and their usefulness grew, spending increased. As product development introduced more and faster items, capital investment in technology companies helped to spawn dramatic business growth. Local economies benefitted differently. In general, suburban and exurban economies grew more rapidly than did urban economies because the skilled technology workers tended to live in those communities.

In the early 1990s, recession hit U.S. communities again, partly fueled by the loss of many manufacturing functions to overseas competitors with considerably lower labor costs. As back-office service functions went overseas, many U.S. communities suffered extraordinary setbacks. Consequently, there was a widening of the gap between "have" and "have not" communities. Again, the general understanding of what constitutes local economic growth needed to be revisited.

Over time, concepts of growth changed to accommodate the reality of development in and around America's cities, and the impacts of those changes were being felt in more rural areas as well. Noteworthy is the shift in the predominance of population growth from the inner to the outer circles. By the end of the 1990s, exurbia accounted for more than 30 percent of the land in the continental United States and accounted for sixty million Americans. "There may soon be more exurbanites than urbanites or inhabitants of central cities."[24]

After a decades-long decline in rural area population, an increase of 1.75 million was recorded between 1989 and 1991; and another 75-percent increase was registered between 1991 and 1994. Many of these migrants to the countryside were highly skilled workers who brought capital with them.[25]

So, what causes communities to grow, and why are the patterns of growth as they are? Madrick argues that markets and information are not the causes of growth, but are simply some of the necessary conditions.[26] Others are education, capital, political stability, and a spirit of entrepreneurialism. He maintains that structures and attitudes must reach certain minimum standards to sustain growth, but that they are not, in and of themselves, the causes of growth.

Madrick maintains that even gross domestic product, or GDP, the sum of all goods and services produced in the nation, is an inadequate metric of growth because it does not reflect the evenness with which such expansion is distributed. More recent measures of gross regional product would have similar limitations, although many economic developers would argue that, within a single region, "a rising tide lifts all ships."

Although some might maintain that the advent of new technologies is a source of growth, Madrick implies that it is as valuable a means of reducing costs as it is of driving new economic growth. Certainly, that is a compelling argument at the regional and local levels of the economy. From the national perspective, Madrick maintains that growth is best measured in the expansion of the workforce and the collective productivity of businesses.[26]

1.4 Births and Deaths of Companies, Industries, and Regions

Over the sixty-plus years since the conclusion of World War II, the sources and locations of economic growth have changed significantly. The consequences of those changes have resulted in the growth and decline of companies, entire industries, and even major regions of the United States.

Areas that had become overly dependent upon a single or relatively few companies or industries were subject to serious economic hardships when the economy negatively affected those companies or industries. The fates of major corporations have resulted in economic ramifications for communities that had once felt impervious to such downturns because those companies were felt to be too solid. But, time and again, communities learned the dangers of a lack of economic diversity.

Later chapters will cover several of these situations and the impacts on the host communities. Strategies used to recover and their ultimate effectiveness will also be discussed. Case studies will be presented of the Seattle experience of the early 1970s when the Boeing Corporation struggled to stay afloat, of Long Island after Grumman laid off 38,000 workers, and the impacts of the declining automobile industry in the Great Lakes region, of oil in Texas, of steel in Pittsburgh, and more.

Not only cities have suffered through the loss of dominant industries. Rural areas have struggled due to the loss of manufacturing functions from the United States to lower-cost markets. This has also occurred with timber and textiles, as well as back-office service functions. The causes and impacts of these losses will be examined in a later chapter as well.

This book will also examine how those cities, towns, and regions have reacted, what was tried, and what worked. It will become clear that sustainability of local economies requires more than simple job growth, and that the ability of local and regional economies to remain secure and vital requires diversification of both industries and companies.

But not all recent local economic history is about where decline and resurgence have occurred. The same changes in national and global economic conditions that have damaged some communities—large and small, rural and urban—have fostered new growth in other markets. Case studies will examine some of these areas to assess what made them grow while other communities and regions were in decline. Are there lessons inherent in these communities' experiences that are transferable to other communities?

In recent years, technology has driven much of the growth in the U.S. economy. However, the growth of technology has also enabled "nontechnology" companies to become faster and more efficient, and their offerings less expensive. But as that efficiency has been reflected in increased productivity rates, so has it spelled job growth in some fields and job losses in others, including manufacturing and distribution. This, in turn, has been translated into uneven gains and losses for U.S. communities.

The industries in which job losses occurred as a result of technology applications have negatively impacted many communities. This, in turn, has resulted in economic disaster for areas where the economies had been dominated by those types of employers. When coupled with the outsourcing trend by American businesses seeking lower costs of production, many communities and regions experienced economic decline throughout some of this nation's fastest and most sustained periods of overall economic growth. A 2003 article in *Business Week* (August 26, 2003) noted that "only a decade ago, writing code and software application maintenance were considered complex and secure ways…to make a living. Now, it is considered 'rote work' and companies such as Microsoft and Netscape have it done everywhere from Ireland to India."

This emphasizes the value of the case studies used in this book. In areas where this type of economic decline was most destructive, communities explored alternative strategies for returning to economic stability. Some of the approaches worked better than others. In the process, much was learned about what does and does not work in specific settings, and why. And a great deal was learned about the process of, and the need for, local economic growth.

1.5 Winners and Losers: Communities at the End of the Twentieth Century

Recent years have seen the growth and decline of different communities throughout the United States. Some of these will be covered in greater depth as case studies. There have been both "winners" and "losers." The winners fall into one of two categories: cities and regions in which new technologies have enabled the growth of companies producing such goods and services; and communities in which the diversification of the economy has enabled it to grow in several directions and protected its stability in downturns either in the economy as a whole or within specific industries.

The cities, towns, and regions that became losers fall into three categories: those in which primary industries have diminished due to legislative missteps, areas in which the labor and production costs have driven the industry to lower-cost markets, and regions in which the decline in fortunes of a dominant employer caused overall economic dislocation.

Fortunately, some of the earlier losers have once again become winners. These, too, will be evaluated for transferable lessons. There is a growing realization that, in the post-industrial economy, knowledge-based industries, companies, and professionals need not be close to customers or other traditional factors. Indeed, they can now locate where they *want* to be rather than where they *need* to be. Once this recognition occurs, one must accept that economic growth is possible anywhere. Indeed, Kotkin refers to the resulting "anti-urban impulse" of some of today's technology workers, emphasizing the changing value of place for today's businesses.[27]

The case studies highlighted in this book will consider who lost and what actions have been taken to turn around the local economies. Rural communities in North Carolina impacted by both decisions about tobacco farming and subsequent natural disasters, regions where state and local policies have driven employers away, and areas that have suffered due to the loss of primary industries to lower-cost markets around the world will be examined.

Among the winners, rapidly growing areas of the southwestern United States come to the top of the list. As manufacturers fled the Rust Belt and headed to the Sun Belt, opportunities arose for the regions that could provide the assets and resources the businesses needed as well as the communities in which their employees could and wanted to live. Those who provided the right kinds of settings and who were clear as to their interest in receiving these businesses have grown. These communities include San Antonio, Phoenix, and others.

Later, as technology-driven companies began to gain market share around the United States and throughout the world, the communities that either had or developed the assets required by those employers saw their economic fortunes increase as well. The location, assets, and amenities of northern Virginia, Austin, Boston, and other areas were the bases for the unprecedented growth of technology companies as well as the overall local and regional economies.

Case studies presented in this book will look at those markets to evaluate the extent to which local policies contributed to the growth and decline of these communities. A special kind of consideration will be the case studies of communities that lost but recovered. What did Pittsburgh do to recover from the loss of the steel industry? Or Seattle in the 1970s, with the cutbacks by Boeing? Or Long Island after the loss of jobs at Grumman? What can others learn to enable similar comebacks elsewhere?

1.6 Twenty-First Century Growth: Do Communities Compete in a Zero-Sum Game?

As the national economy grows, there are winners and losers. At the same time, there will be cities and regions that benefit from that growth and those that will not. Is it possible for all communities to grow, or is there a finite amount of growth which, once exhausted, cannot be gained elsewhere without moving from one place to the next?

Some economists argue that the competition for business attraction among communities is a zero-sum game: from the national perspective, twenty jobs equals twenty jobs whether they stay in California or relocate to Ohio. This is not entirely true. Companies move for good reasons: if, by relocating an office or other facility, the business can become more efficient, the ultimate yield may be additional jobs.

Moreover, not all observers agree that local economic growth is a zero-sum game. Although "one of the criticisms of local development efforts is that cities compete without increasing the number of jobs" and that "one community gains at the expense of another," business incentives could have the effect of increasing output and efficiency, thereby enabling additional job creation.[28] It should also be noted that relocation could bring a company closer to inputs, labor force, or transportation options that would also have the effect of increasing efficiency, resulting in an increased level of jobs.

However, regardless of whether the larger economy benefits from corporate relocations, some communities will. The residents of some regions will have more job opportunities and the small businesses of some regions will have opportunities to make new sales. And some municipalities can enhance their real estate and sales tax bases and thus improve the public services that constitute the overall quality of life for their residents or, alternatively, reduce the residential tax rates or both. Brunori concurs: local governments must "promote and protect the wealth of their citizens. Local governments do so by competing with other areas to attract firms and individuals who will contribute more in taxes than they will consume in services, protective zoning practices, and the provision of higher level public services at modest tax costs."[29]

Almost certainly at any given time, there is a finite amount of growth. There is only so much financing available, only so much entrepreneurial spirit and business acumen, only so many good minds. As companies grow, they create jobs and develop facilities to accommodate the contracts they have in hand and the business they expect to receive. They will not likely develop new plants and offices or hire additional staff beyond their forecasted needs. Once they have reached the extent of their need, they will stop growing until their needs change.

Shaffer writes that "communities compete for limited resources…the competition occurs as communities try to position themselves as a location with a comparative advantage."[30] But Cortright counters that economic development is not a zero-sum game because today's knowledge-based industries have no real limitations to the amount of new ideas and growth they can generate.[31] Although it is true that growth could conceivably continue into the future unabated, at any specific point in time there will be a finite number of business relocations and expansions to pursue.

Given that there is not unlimited growth at any given time, communities that need to establish and sustain economic stability must be aggressive in its pursuit. Professionals in the field of economic development will attest to the fact that theirs is a highly competitive profession. If the business prospect locates in another area, they do not locate in theirs. In states where public services are provided on the basis of local income taxes, this may not be a problem if the location is nearby. In such instances, residents of many communities may get jobs and small businesses from throughout the region may get contracts to provide goods and services. But that is a function of distance.

However, in states where local governments rely largely on real estate taxes to fund public services, the matter is quite different. Consider the case of Fairfax County, Virginia, where 24 percent of all income taxes in the Commonwealth of Virginia come from Fairfax County alone. But as less than twenty cents on every dollar are returned by the state in the form of programs and infrastructure projects, the Fairfax County Board of Supervisors relies heavily on real estate taxes to fund its schools, libraries, parks, public safety, and other public services. Nearly two-thirds of the $3.7 billion general fund comes from real estate taxes. By growing the local economy, Fairfax County has been able to generate a large tax base from the business community, resulting in a declining tax rate for residents: from $1.74 in fiscal year 1976 to $1.42 in FY1984 to $0.92 in FY2009.

In cases like that of Fairfax County, business growth represents a zero-sum situation as applied to the tax base, but not in terms of job-seekers and small businesses in neighboring localities. Nonetheless, it needs to be very clear that economic development is a highly competitive endeavor. And that applies both to business attraction as well as business retention. Communities need to provide not only what will make businesses decide to come, but also what is needed by existing businesses to remain in the community and grow.

Even within the context of competition between communities for relocating firms, the results can often be seen as a search for the environment most conducive to operating effectively. If one accepts that the result can be efficiencies for the employer, it is reasonable to conclude that the end result could be increases in production, jobs, and expenditures as well as overall contributions to the state and local tax coffers.

1.7 A Working Definition of Local Economic Growth

Each locality has a different economic history and different needs, assets, and interests for its economic growth. Therefore, the definition of local economic growth must be, at once, broad enough to be inclusive, yet narrow enough to retain focus on the relevant needs and issues.

Another requirement of a working definition is that it must keep the focus of this analysis on the factors that are truly relevant to the study of local economic growth. A wide range of activities support local economic growth. For example, O'Sullivan cites six such factors as relates to urban economic growth: market forces, land use, transportation networks, crime and public policy, housing, and municipal tax policies and expenditures.[32]

Conversely, any definition should highlight, as clearly as possible, that which is not pertinent. Thus, for the purpose of this text, local economic growth shall be understood to mean the expansion and stability of the job base and financial benefits to the labor force and businesses as well as to the city, county, region, or other catchment area accessible to or dependent upon those employers and related commercial activities.

1.8 The Relevance of Economic Growth to Today's Communities and Leadership

To say that economic growth at the local level leads to jobs, taxes, and wealth generation is unnecessary. However, the local economy is more than simply a source of income and tax revenues. Communities that enjoy stable economies develop a spirit. They are places to which people want to move. They are places in which the quantity *and* the quality of public education and other public services can be enhanced because the wherewithal exists to do so. And those things can be provided for the residents of those communities without placing the entire burden of the costs on residents.

A strong business base means that the community can have strong and viable institutions. A community that has a stable economy can support not only the essentials of community life, but also the organizations that constitute an improvement in the overall quality of life in a city, town, or region. This might include the symphony, ball fields and recreational opportunities, better libraries and parks, or social services to assist the less fortunate.

Economic stability translates into the kind of community of which people are proud. In short, it promotes community pride; and often, pride in one's community leads to greater citizen involvement. Clearly, this is good for the community itself; but it is also good for the elected officials of the community. They are able to provide the public services their constituents demand and deserve; and they are able to establish a certain enthusiasm about life in their communities.

As the business base grows, especially in the creative areas of the economy, there grows an enhanced demand and support for lifestyle enhancements. Outdoor or arts and cultural opportunities may become more prevalent. This may include theaters and concert halls, museums and orchestras, or bike trails and ball fields. Businesses also cause the growth of both business and personal services companies. Business growth generates additional clients for existing companies. They increase the use of hotels, meeting space, and restaurants. They use stationers and caterers and accounting and legal services.

Friedman makes note of these noneconomic impacts of growth: "Not only does a better standard of living come to seem familiar and customary, so too do changes like improved working conditions, fewer hours on the job, and superior medical treatment. Only if growth and change persist will people continue to feel better off."[33] Economic growth is seen as leading to overall community betterment. The next chapter will deal with how community officials can merge their plans for economic growth with other local planning and programs.

1.9 Concluding Thoughts

The concept of economic growth changes with time, location, and community characteristics. It is more or less welcome, depending on the time and place. Sometimes it is aggressively pursued, sometimes opposed; often it is simply tolerated. Given the increasingly clear nexus between local economic growth and the ability of municipal governments to provide the expected quality, quantity, and scope of public services, communities have become more intent upon securing it than ever before. This has caused the competition between communities for essentially finite growth opportunities to intensify.

As the competition continues to increase, some localities will improve their economic sustainability and growth outlook while others will decline; but none will stand still. Some of those outcomes are avoidable or manageable, others are not. Local elected officials must make decisions about what their constituencies need and want, how best to pursue it, and how to live with the consequences. There are, of course, limits to what local governments can influence. National and global economic forces are beyond local control. But, as Cisneros wrote, that "does not mean that local and regional leaders must simply sit back and await their market-determined fate."[34] Local economic growth must be pursued and, as the competition for that growth heats up, localities must become increasingly aggressive in its pursuit.

Economic growth at the local level has been viewed differently and has had varied impacts in localities over time. Following World War II, the changing nature of economic growth caused substantial changes in the very physical nature of this country. Some cities and some regions grew while others declined. New regions grew quite literally out of the desert. The nature of farming has changed. The nature of manufacturing has changed. Suburbs grew and began to take on economic roles previously accorded to the center cities. The resulting new economic paradigm has meant that the very basis of how we regard community has also changed. Our horizons as residents of the world are different. We are more mobile as a society, and form different expectations of our environments. Those expectations depend either directly or indirectly on the ability to find employment and the various services and amenities that come from economic growth.

Some of the expectations we have collectively may be unreasonable, but we still want them. We want jobs, but not congested roads; we want to generate taxes and create wealth, but we want to be able to control any environmental impacts. However, communities may have to compromise from the ideal of what they want either to obtain or preserve. As Atkinson and Andes point out, in the last decade, 30 percent of the job growth in the United States occurred in just five states.[35] Other communities are beginning to see the need for increasingly active efforts to attract employers and grow the local economy. To do so, and to thereby provide constituents with the public services they need and expect, may ultimately mean that cities, counties, and regions will have to accept a certain level of congestion, a little more environmental impacts than ideally wanted, and perhaps others of the negative aspects of local economic growth. Like all things in local politics, economic growth is a question of options and choices. Local elected officials seek a creative balance that takes maximum advantage of the benefits of local growth, while restricting its unwanted consequences. The solutions may be less than perfect and local governments may be in positions to accept the lesser of the evils presented to them.

And, of course, many communities are now in pursuit of the finite opportunities for business relocations. Only new business growth and support for business expansions can provide significant net new job growth. And this is where communities tend to focus much of their economic development efforts. Indeed, economic growth becomes increasingly engrained in the overall structure and operation of the community, as will be seen in the next chapter.

Notes

1. Cisneros, "Urban Entrepreneurialsim and National Economic Growth," 55.
2. Bean and Leach, "A Critical Disjuncture?," 64.
3. Downs, *New Visions*, vii.
4. Ibid., vii.
5. "The Post War Economy: 1945–1960," http://www.economics.about.com/od/useconomichistory/a/post_war.htm.
6. Hudnut, *Cities on the Rebound*, 114. Hudnut argues that the growth of suburbs and the resurgence of enthusiasm for normality in America following the war contributed to the decline of cities that continued over several decades.
7. Bingham and Mier, *Theories of Economic Development*, 33. This notion that cities will make a comeback because they can leapfrog outmoded technologies that they do not have and go straight to the latest technology should be considered as a contributing factor to economic growth only. Other factors, such as public safety, good schools, and the quality of labor force, receive greater credence from business site location decision makers. A strong case for the impacts of cutting-edge technology being a primary factor is more difficult to make or to find in the literature.
8. "House of Cards: Las Vegas—Too Many People in the Wrong Place, Celebrating as a Way of Life," http://www.radicalurbantheory.com/davis/housecards.html.
9. Gillham, *The Limitless City*, 41.
10. Ibid., 41.
11. Downs, *New Visions*, 4.
12. Cisneros, "Urban Entrepreneurialism," 10.
13. Flint, *This Land*, 2.

14. Marshall, *How Cities Work*, xv. The so-called "edge cities" have indeed become, in some cases, primary job centers while the cities supply the labor force. The U.S. Department of Labor has often noted this to be the case in the Washington, D.C., suburb of Fairfax County, Virginia, where the primary jobs market, especially among private-sector employers, has long exceeded the employment base of the city itself.
15. O'Sullivan, *Urban Economics*, 72.
16. Gillham, *The Limitless City*, 39.
17. O'Toole, *The Vanishing Automobile*, 19.
18. Bruegmann, *Sprawl*, 80.
19. Hudnut, *Cities on the Rebound*, 108.
20. Fruth, "The Flow of Money and Its Impact on Local Economies," 6.
21. Bruegmann, *Sprawl*, 58.
22. Ibid., 87. The outward-to-inward commuting patterns are clearly evidenced in suburban Fairfax County, Virginia, where nearly half of the 600,000+ jobs are filled by in-migrating workers every day.
23. Hudnut, *Cities on the Rebound*, 108.
24. Bruegmann, *Sprawl*, 87.
25. Kotkin, *The New Geography*, 45.
26. Madrick, *Why Economies Grow*, 30.
27. Kotkin, *The New Geography*, 27–51.
28. Bingham and Mier, *Theories of Economic Development*, 15. It is reasonable to argue that the efficiencies created by relocating businesses may generate additional employment opportunities and thus justify the use of incentives to enable those relocations. However, the literature overwhelmingly argues that the use of incentives is aimed at job creation for communities and not greater efficiencies for the beneficiary companies.
29. Brunori, *Local Tax Policy*, 8.
30. Shaffer, *Community Economics*, 144.
31. Cortright, "New Growth Theory, Technology, and Learning: A Practitioner Guide," 25.
32. O'Sullivan, *Urban Economics*, 72.
33. Friedman, *Moral Consequences of Economic Growth*, 83.
34. Cisneros, "Urban Entrepreneurialsim," 55.
35. Atkinson and Andes, "The 2008 State New Economy Index," 6.

Chapter 2

Viewing Economic Growth as Part of a Comprehensive Community Strategy

2.1 Introduction

Communities' economies evolve over time as events in the surrounding environments cause change—either growth or contraction. That change will occur over time—even in the absence of planning or efforts to pursue it—that much is inevitable. The adaptation by municipalities and regions of the practice of strategic planning that has its origins in the business world gives testimony to this certainty. Community leaders recognize the need to identify what's approaching and either how to avoid it, manage it, or best to react to it; this includes commercial and residential development, economic trends, and their related impacts. As communities examine these issues intensely, the nexus between strategic planning for economic growth and stability and other municipal or regional concerns has become increasingly clear.

Communities and regions have now long engaged in a variety of forms of planning that are designed to control that change to the extent possible, rather than simply accepting what may come naturally. Planning for land use, financial management, and other local government functions often overlap and sometimes conflict. In the worst applications, the various elements of municipal planning take place absent any coordination of the component parts.

Effective coordination of various elements of municipal planning may be evidenced in various forms. It may involve the comprehensive alignment of all plans as separate components woven into a larger, single plan; or it may mean the consistent coordination of separate plans that have been prepared in conjunction but are implemented distinctly; or it may mean the coordination of plans by independent jurisdictions across the breadth of a metropolitan area. Cookie-cutter approaches do not work, but the lessons learned from the experiences of some can provide benefits to others.

Planning by cities or regions for the growth of the local economy must be consistent with the designs of the local land use plans. This is especially difficult for regions in which economic development is coordinated by a regional entity, but the land use applications are not. Neighboring jurisdictions often identify distinctly different industries for outreach that require distinctly different land uses. Although a manufacturing facility, for example, may be well suited within the borders of one community, if it is contiguous to a residential area in the neighboring community, there could arise conflicts between the uses. This argues for intrajurisdictional planning coordination in many functional areas including the interjurisdictional coordination of planning for economic growth.

2.2 Static Growth: If Communities Do Not Grow, Do They Die?

Imagine a continuum, along which various degrees of local economic growth are plotted, ranging from total demise to the most extreme pace of growth. At the midpoint, one would locate an absolutely static economy: no growth, no contraction. All measures of economic activity would remain at rest: local or regional product would stay the same, the job base would not expand or shrink, and expendable income would exactly keep pace with inflation. This point for a community, or an entire region, is an imaginary place. One small change in any relevant metric of the economy, or the growth of the population or changes in the demographics of the community, would cause ripples to occur through others, thus spreading the fact and pace of change. Moreover, as other communities grow, one's own comparative position, in the absence of any momentum of its own, must be considered to be diminished.

The conclusion must be that an absolutely static economy is fiction. Logically, then, local and regional economies, starting from one point on the continuum, have but two possible futures: either their economic position will improve or it will decline. As has already been discussed, there is a finite potential for economic growth at any given point in time. The result has been that communities have become increasingly aggressive about pursuing economic growth. After all, to a great extent, there will only be so much growth to be had, and other cities and regions are also pursuing whatever growth may occur.

Communities have thus become increasingly aggressive about competing for the economic growth that will occur. Morfesis noted (*Phoenix Business Journal,* December 31, 2006) that it was the 1980s that "witnessed governors becoming activists in the economic development of their states. More than thirty states created strategic plans for economic development during that decade." This increased emphasis on economic growth will, for some, mean the development and implementation of strategies to grow indigenous businesses. For many, it will also mean the pursuit of growth of the local economy employment base through the attraction of company expansions or relocations. Not to compete is not to win. Not to win some of the opportunities will mean that there will be limited economic growth in the community and that there may even be decline. Economic growth planning becomes a major consideration in all other forms of municipal planning and operations because at least some of what is planned will be dependent on who comes, who stays, and who leaves.

It is clear that nothing in the economy can be taken for granted. The case studies considered in this book clearly illustrate that what is at once assumed to be a stable economic foundation for future generations can be lost very quickly. The importance of diversifying the local industrial/commercial base and the base of primary employers were lessons learned painfully by those in Pittsburgh (steel), Seattle (Boeing), and other locations. In an article in the Houston press, Schadewald confirmed that, "if the '80s taught Houston anything, it's that the most robust economy can be rapidly followed by a dramatic reversal of fortune" (*Houston Business Journal*, March 8, 1998). Indeed, it can happen anywhere and at any time, and it has often occurred as the consequence of stunning reversals of companies that had hitherto been considered so solid that the community would forever be secure.

Communities are unlikely to remain in a static economic position. Too much is changing all around them. They will either see their local economic fortunes rise or decline. The questions for local leaders are simply: What kind of growth is desirable? How much? How best to control that growth and its effects? Economic growth is a highly competitive endeavor, as will be seen later. If neighboring communities are growing while yours is not, the result is not a static position, but rather a relative decline. Even modest growth may be insufficient to enable a community to maintain its quality of life. As residential numbers increase, the growth of the business community becomes increasingly important because it enables local governments to provide public services while minimizing the tax burdens for residents. If growth of the commercial tax base cannot keep pace with the growth of the residential sector and its resultant demand for public services, the community has not maintained its economic position; it has declined.

2.3 Building Economic Growth into the Master Plan

As communities have increased the level of their economic development outreach, they have developed analyses of what types of businesses they wish to pursue and evaluated the assets they possess to attract those businesses. Once that has been accomplished, planners need to identify the existing properties and structures suitable to the needs as well as the potential for new sites to accommodate the desired level and types of growth. These requirements must be incorporated into land use plans to permit the attraction and accommodation of businesses. The incorporation of these amendments into the Master Land Use Plan enables local elected and administrative officials to consider all relevant policies that need to be enacted or revised to support the pursuit of these plans.

Two reasons have become more important than ever in recent years. The first relates to the threat of terrorism and the resultant requirements for some federal office space and other facilities. These may require internal or external fortifications, setbacks from public thoroughfares, and other security measures. The second trend in business attraction and retention that is critical for land use planners relates to new requirements for, and interest in, the construction and retrofitting of buildings and other facilities to be more consistent with "green" standards for energy consumption and preservation.

A report prepared by the Office of the State Comptroller in New York states the relationship between various forms of local planning this way: "Local fiscal conditions are driven by local tax bases and service needs, both of which are heavily affected by the type of development that occurs. Development patterns drive the creation and maintenance of public infrastructure, and the efficiency of transportation and government services. Economic growth is dependent, among other things, on the availability of property for occupation or development, transportation systems, and local taxes."[1]

Local officials possess a variety of instruments that can either hinder or enable growth in their communities. In different states, different tools are more or less available and can be more or less effective. Of course, the practices of land use planning can differ widely from one area to the next. In Houston, for example, the strong emphasis on individualism and an unrestrained free market economy has resulted in "the lack of government planning and land use controls in the city...Voters in Houston have rejected zoning twice, and the city council blocked implementation two other times...Without a strong city planning department and without the land use controls of other American cities, the public sector has allowed businessmen to plan the city through the profit mechanism. This investment planning has resulted in a sprawling, low-density city, linked by a massive freeway system that delineates city sectors."[2] Although this has allowed Houston to develop as it wished, such a dearth of formal public controls might not work in many other areas. Hevesi noted, however, that "comprehensive planning is a very good way to review a community's land use strategy in a smart growth context. Many communities in (New York

State) do not have comprehensive plans (about 40 percent, according to a 1999 study); among those that do have plans, most were prepared decades ago and are severely out of date."[3]

Generally, local officials have at their disposal two types of powers to affect growth other than economic development marketing. They can either control the extent, pace, and types of growth through the land use planning and zoning processes or they can utilize a variety of legal, regulatory, and practical mechanisms that can either facilitate and stimulate growth, or impede or decelerate it.

Through the land use practices of local governments, elected officials can dictate more than the permitted uses and densities of various parcels; they can also control the value of property in and around a locality. By controlling the amount of land available for specific uses, the supply of that land becomes scarce, thus providing upward pressure on the price. By controlling what land is designated as zoned for development, localities can determine where businesses will locate and grow and what open spaces will be preserved. By designating lands for commercial development, a community's leadership expresses a conscious decision to pursue or allow economic growth.

Some maintain that land use planning is too often overly restrictive. The mayor of Anaheim, California, argued in 2007 that "too many government officials want to dictate how and when development takes place. Sadly, many of these grand plans fail."[4] Of course, many communities do want to control where things are built and what is done with their lands; and many local land use plans have good or excellent success in creating workable, livable environments.

But community planning encompasses more than the governance of land usage. Plans abound for transportation, housing, parks and open space, and more. The challenge for localities is coordination; and this means intrajurisdictionally as well as interjurisdictionally. Within the community, planners must ensure that all plans are consistent and compatible. Because different staffs have different responsibilities, and because there are often different citizen advisory panels for each functional area, it is relatively easy to imagine a situation in which plans can be internally valid but, at the same time, in conflict with other forms of planning for the same area.

In the last fifty years of the twentieth century, the population of Phoenix grew at a tremendous rate, creating demand for housing and jobs. However, much of that growth "occurred during a period when the region lacked a long-term regional economic strategy, resulting in the same type of transportation and congestion problems, housing price increases, and internecine fighting between city and governmental agencies that characterized similar periods of economic growth in Silicon Valley in the early 1990s and the central Puget Sound region in the late 1990s and early 2000s."[5]

An especially challenging area of coordination takes place in multijurisdictional metropolitan areas. To some extent, a municipality's land use plans for border areas are dependent upon the planning by neighboring jurisdictions for contiguous border areas. In the absence of such coordination, mismatched uses can occur among immediate neighbors simply because they are incidentally part of distinct land use practices and philosophies.

And, of course, many matters beyond land use have interjurisdictional implications, including taxing districts, sewer and water treatment, transportation, environmental concerns, and more. Jane Jacobs wrote that "the work of city planning commissioners and their staffs seldom deals with a big city as a total organism. In truth, because of the nature of the work to be done, almost all city planning is concerned with relatively small and specific acts, done here and done there, in specific streets, neighborhoods, and districts."[6]

As communities grow, and as regions emerge, greater coordination becomes critical. These are the planning challenges for local officials: consistency, comprehensiveness, compatibility, and cooperation. And all of this often takes place within the context of heated competition for economic growth.

2.4 Theoretical Foundations for Local Economic Growth

A variety of theories have been presented over the years to explain why economic growth does or does not occur, and why it does in some places rather than others. This seems entirely appropriate because, as has been discussed, local economic growth is, at least in part, a function of local conditions, the point in time, and a broad range of external factors. Further, over time, the causes and effects of growth have changed as industries and mankind's collective knowledge have changed. One question for this work is whether a synthesis can be derived from all of these theories that would serve to explain all—or even most—situations. In other words, could there be a general model of local economic growth? To address this question, one must consider the available theoretical constructs that seek to explain local economic growth.

One of the more basic theories of economic growth is referred to as location theory. This posits that companies locate in close proximity to their markets to minimize delivery costs and maximize their profits. As Stimson et al. point out, "much of the focus has been on transport costs, labor costs, other production costs, scale of operation."[7] This is essentially the expression of the old bromide "location, location, location," and may appear on the surface to be more applicable to manufacturing-based economies than those involved with the service sectors.

Location, however, is a key ingredient in bringing service companies to a community. The relative success of recruiting and keeping a qualified workforce in a given location is dependent upon the presence of educational institutions and a variety of lifestyle options. Location theory suggests that value is derived by corporate decision makers by the ease of access to a wide range of factors required for corporate success. Location theory "evolved from simple transportation cost-minimization models. As the theory progressed, spatial variations in market size, production and cost differentials, regional amenities, technological capabilities, and other factors were integrated into increasingly complex models of the industrial location decision process."[8]

Indeed, many cities have succeeded in growing the local economy because they are either at the transportation receiving end or near the delivery end of the network, thus reducing on-loading and off-loading times and costs. It is also noted, however, that "more recent empirical studies indicate that, as the economy and technology became more complex, the list of significant location factors has been lengthened" while traditional basic cost factors "have declined in relative importance."[9]

Some of the more critical location factors have been examined thoroughly as they have increased in relative importance. Shaffer illuminates most succinctly the neoclassical theory of economic growth originally purported by Solow and others. The key is that, as profits increase, so does the level of savings. Those savings serve as "a pool of funds used to finance investments. These investments fuel the accumulation of new capital."[10] This theory begins to explain the value of venture capital and angel investments in communities as well as the use of public pensions to invest in start-ups in the community.

The neoclassical model also suggests that increases in the factors of production, which are understood to include the advance and application of technology, create efficiencies in production. This begins to lead us to an explanation of why some communities grow faster than others: they simply possess the factors that are in greatest demand in the greatest amounts. However, Shaffer points out that, as technologies advance, they can cause an increase in jobs or a decrease, depending on the nature of the efficiencies created.[11] This means that the communities that grow may be the ones that possess or obtain or develop not the most recent technological advances, but the next ones.

Endogenous and exogenous growth theories advance the notion that, although an area is susceptible to external factors that impact local growth, it is still possible for local forces to sustain growth. Stimson et al. include in that grouping of forces leadership and institutions, physical infrastructure, and human capital.[12] Because such factors will be more effective in sustaining economic growth over a larger area, with more diverse factors, the endogenous and exogenous theories may be more relevant to considerations of why and how regions grow rather than cities, towns, counties, or rural areas.

The product cycle, or innovation cycle, theory emphasizes that products pass through cycles that mirror human life. They are incubated, grow, and ultimately decline and pass out of use, having been replaced by the next generation of product or innovation. This is not dissimilar to the neoclassical model in that it begins to explain why some communities' growth may outpace growth in other areas. Again, it is the community that is not dominated by the older technology, or the later cycles of a product's life, that will sustain its economic growth. In much the same way that younger people may be more employable in some technology companies than their older counterparts due to their greater technology capabilities, the communities that will enjoy economic stability are those that are the source of the next advance in a product or the next innovation. As Shaffer wrote, "even in the decline phase, improved technology may enable a community's producers to capture an increasing share of the stagnant industry's sales and thus contribute to an expansion of the community's economic growth."[13]

Two additional theories of economic growth deserve greater attention at this juncture. The first is known as economic base theory which, in its simplest form, argues that a region grows if its businesses export their goods and services outside of the area. When that occurs, money comes into the local economy and is spent and re-spent. Blair and Premus explain that the "economic activities of a region can be divided between industries producing goods for export to other regions and industries producing goods or services for local consumption." Their conclusion is that "the economic development of a region depends on its ability to raise the volume of exports relative to consumption of locally produced goods and services."[14] Similarly, retirees who receive pensions from sources outside the area are importers of capital that circulates throughout the community, which creates a multiplier effect. The value of this theory relates to communities that are analyzing the industries for which they have strengths and which they intend to pursue. These theories may be useful in helping to point communities toward the assets that need to be developed, whether that means capital, a skilled labor force, or other business and quality of life factors, and supports the applications of the gap analysis that will be covered in a later chapter.

Finally, there is new-growth theory, which emphasizes the correlation between the advance of technology and the growth of local economies. This is an important consideration for this book as it asserts that communities can foster additional growth by acquiring and helping to evolve businesses that are knowledge-intensive rather than land-, capital-, or labor-intensive. Such industries put less stress on the environment and community resources than trade industry sectors, while contributing more stable and better paying jobs to the community. The question for communities then becomes how, within their targeted industries, to develop, attract, and enhance knowledge and apply it to business processes or products. This also relates closely to the work on creative economies by Richard Florida, which will be covered later in this chapter, as well as Michael Porter's prolific writing on the subject of business clusters, which will be covered in a later chapter in this book.

As to the question posed at the beginning of this section—can there be a general model of local economic growth?—one has to conclude that, although there is no one-size-fits-all solution, there are certain theoretical foundations to any practical plan for local economic growth. As one might expect, these conclusions can be classified either as things to do or things to avoid.

2.5 Public Policies for Economic Growth: Dos and Don't-Dos

Public policy decisions can intentionally or unintentionally influence the effectiveness of plans for local economic growth. Communities can, however, design policies that will enhance the availability and quality of the public services that will lead to an overall improvement in the quality of life. This can, in turn, increase the likelihood that businesses will want to locate there. Many communities and many local elected officials have concluded that this is a far better approach to encouraging local economic growth than is the provision of tax holidays or other economic development location incentives to businesses.

There is, however, a fine line for local governments to walk. Bradbury et al. wrote that "tax incentives can foster development by reducing business costs, but can also indirectly impede development if they reduce expenditures on public services that businesses value. Similarly, deregulation may cut the costs of production, but it can also diminish the attractiveness of a location if it causes deterioration in environmental quality."[15]

One area in which local officials can be very effective is in building local coalitions. A U.S. Department of Labor publication notes that "visionary communities increasingly appear to be led by broadened civic leadership that includes higher education; philanthropic and health sectors; economic development professionals willing to think 'out of the box' and concerned about results; industry; and finally, supportive state and local governments interested in partnering with…not driving the agenda."[16] Such collaborations do not just occur; they must be created and nurtured.

The motivation for the economic growth of core cities may be different from those of their suburban neighbors. Cities need to attract jobs for inner city residents, but must do so against a range of factors that generally deter businesses from considering locations. "The high crime rates and other forces that caused businesses to abandon these neighborhoods in the first place will prevent them from being lured back. And, such additional factors as shortages of large vacant sites for modern plants and warehouses, high insurance costs, and a long-range trend toward decentralization of all types of activities reinforce their choice."[17] Furthermore, "the poor quality of public schooling in inner cities aggravates all the other problems. It handicaps young people trying to get good jobs, which drives many into illegal activities."[18] The agenda for cities trying to attract business is clear. Businesses will locate where the climate best suits their needs. This often means that localities must first improve conditions before implementing aggressive economic development campaigns.

In some cases, municipalities need to simplify regulatory and developmental processes to attract or retain businesses. The *Puget Sound Business Journal* noted that "Seattle's consensus-driven, process-intensive politics compromise its ability to accomplish anything quickly. On the regional level, big civic projects such as light rail or new airport runways often bog down in protracted disputes. According to

Wilhelm, the uncertainty of action on vital issues…Boeing has said, is one of the factors that led it to look elsewhere (for its corporate headquarters location)—and may force the company to move manufacturing jobs out of Washington" (*Puget Sound Business Journal*, May 17, 2002). Blair and Premus have confirmed this: "it is not the level of state and local regulations that concern businesses as it is uncertainty over future regulatory policies."[19]

By comparison, Chicago, the city to which the headquarters was moved, in Wilhelm's perception, "bustles with power. It's run from the top by a tight coalition of businessmen, politicians, and even labor leaders, with a tradition of accomplishing what they decide to do" (*Puget Sound Business Journal*, May 17, 2002). Clearly, there is a lesson for community leaders in the importance of smooth and efficient governance as well as strong political–business cooperation, to the business community.

Much of the existing literature in the field promotes the development of the "business climate" as an economic growth strategy. This is a critical conclusion based on the assumption that a more attractive business location is one that possesses certain assets that are important to commerce in general. These may include the following:

■ The preparation of an available and highly qualified labor pool.
■ The availability of basic education and training and retraining opportunities for specific industries and job descriptions.
■ Local governments and public services that are effective and efficient.
■ Transportation networks that are consistent with the needs of the companies for the movement of people and goods.
■ An openness to people of various backgrounds and perspectives.
■ A fair tax system for businesses.
■ A comprehensive but not burdensome structure of regulatory requirements for businesses.
■ The means of accomplishing the transfer of technology from schools, laboratories, and individuals to the point of commercialization.
■ The establishment of business networks that enable the transfer of ideas, capital, contracts, and labor.
■ The creation and encouragement of business organizations and their close alliance with the public sector.
■ A variety and availability of housing stock.
■ A high quality of life in an attractive and welcoming community.

Increasingly, the quality of public education has assumed a vital role in business attraction and retention. A publication of the National Education Association quite correctly points out that residents and businesses both "prefer to locate in areas with comparatively better schools. Increased education spending makes a community a more desirable place to live and work and thus more people move there. An increase in the region's attractiveness also means that workers will be more willing to accept employment in the area."[20] This is especially true for technology businesses, which can only succeed if they are able to attract and retain employees with strong technology skills. These men and women have themselves been very well trained and expect the same for their children. This gives communities with the strongest public education systems a competitive advantage over other areas.

Arts and cultural advantages also make a community more livable and more conducive to business growth—both attraction and retention. Several of the case study cities cited later in this book (e.g., Austin and Phoenix) are frequently cited as strong examples of these quality-of-life features. Stanton wrote that "there is a growing awareness in Phoenix of the arts in terms of economic impact, downtown and neighborhood revitalization, tourism, business attraction and retention, and enhancing our community's overall quality of life." He also notes that, "in addition to recognizing the economic impact of the arts, the arts play an important role in attracting knowledge workers to our (Phoenix) community" (*Phoenix Business Journal*, May 9, 2007). Senator Edward Kennedy has further pointed out that "the arts benefit communities as well as individuals. Cities and towns with flourishing cultural activities attract businesses and tourists and provide tremendous incentives for families…They have strengthened their economies and greatly improved the quality of life in their neighborhoods."[21]

Although much will be written herein about ensuring local economic diversification away from single dominant industries or employers, that is not to say that local elected officials ought not to support those industries/employers as well. The economic development professionals in the Puget Sound region, for example, have collectively acknowledged that "a healthy Boeing is central to any overall plan to restore economic vitality…in short, we must do for Boeing what Europe and France do for Airbus. We, the people and taxpayers of the state and the region, will be the beneficiaries through the availability of high wage jobs and the tax base that supports public services…We will benefit from a higher quality of life as well. When we lose Boeing workers, we lose neighbors, community volunteers, Little League coaches, and much more" (*Puget Sound Business Journal*, May 9, 2003).

Local officials must constantly scan economic development strategies to ensure consistency between those plans and a wide variety of local ordinances that could either enable or hinder the growth that has been imagined. Land use has already been mentioned, but other potential areas of municipal governance must also be considered, including tax policies, environmental controls, incentive programs, and use of the right of eminent domain. As Anthony Downs adds, "city governments should make special efforts to discover what such firms need and meet those needs with a minimum of bureaucratic delay and red tape…the best way for local governments to meet their needs would be to perform their normal functions in a more responsive manner."[22] And Conklin wrote that Oregon's Silicon Forest, for example, was felt to be the result of "a number of key public policy decisions that encouraged capital investment and economic growth, created an efficient transportation infrastructure to serve both commuters and commerce, and provided workable land use policies" (*Portland Business Journal*, April 8, 2005). Local government policies and processes can either enable or retard economic growth, and there are several tools at the disposal of local officials to take them in those directions.

2.5.1 Tax Policies

Tax policies are a particularly difficult area to coordinate. Knowing that tax considerations are important to site location decision makers but seldom the primary consideration, local officials must implement policies and rates that are at once friendly to business while not appearing to be so at the expense of residents. At the same time, they must ensure the generation of sufficient marginal tax revenues to offset the costs of any additional infrastructure or other public services that result from the growth of the local business community.

Elected officials will pursue business growth, at least in part, to generate the additional tax revenues that provide the enhanced public education and other public services that encouraged the community to accept and pursue economic growth in the first place. It is indeed a fine balancing act to collect additional tax revenues while convincing economic development prospects that the community is business-friendly. There are numerous examples of communities that have overreached in their efforts to benefit from local growth and "killed the goose that laid the golden egg" in the process.

Vedder wrote, in 2003, that one need only compare states' tax decisions and observe the effects to see their relative benefit to sustained local economic growth. Compare Virginia, he wrote, with Ohio. "In 1970, Ohio's per capita income exceeded Virginia's by about seven percent. Today, Virginia outdistances Ohio on this important measure by about eleven percent. Why? In part, because Ohio retrogressed from being a relatively low tax state to a relatively high tax state, while Virginia did not."[23] Other examples will be described in detail in later case studies.

Community leaders must also pay great attention to extant environmental controls and the concerns of the local citizenry. Another delicate balancing act comes when trying to decide whether a manufacturing process that does not fit the limits imposed by local ordinances should be turned away. When the economy is strong and residents are employed, such decisions may be quite different from those made when the economy is in decline and the unemployment rate is soaring.

This is not to say that elected officials can be cavalier or inattentive when the situation justifies it, but there is sometimes a natural inclination to regard immediate human needs first and the environment later. For planners, it represents yet another case in which the various plans of a city or county or region must be closely coordinated and understood.

2.5.2 Incentive Programs

Many communities employ state or local incentive programs to attract and retain the businesses that will grow and sustain the economy. These may include loans or tax rebates, deductions, credits, or even outright grants or gifts of cash, land, or facilities. This is a very treacherous practice; once begun, it becomes extremely difficult to agree to tax abatements or outright grants in some situations, but not to do so in others.

The practice is, to a considerable extent, promulgated by real estate brokers and site location consultants who advertise their experience and expertise in finding communities that will give companies the best offers to locate within their borders. Their concern lies not with the communities, but rather with their clients and their own self-interest. In many cases, their fees are based, at least in part, on the value of the incentive packages they are able to negotiate with job-hungry communities.

Peters and Fisher estimated in 2004 that there was about $50 billion in current incentive agreements outstanding.[24] However, many economic development professionals feel that incentive agreements have a place only for either exceptional prospect situations or for areas which are at such extraordinary economic disadvantage that no other strategy can be effective in attracting employers. Even then, the assumption is typically that it is the state's responsibility, rather than the locality's, to provide the necessary resources. Of course, even those agreements must be carefully structured to benefit all parties and not to leave the public's investment unprotected.

To avoid such circumstances, communities usually establish criteria that address the expected return on investment and use those standards as the means to say yes or no. Such guidelines only serve to make the decision more mechanical and often tie officials' hands when they might otherwise wish to decline such a "deal."

Some observers argue that the practice of granting economic development incentives is now so pervasive that communities often feel compelled to engage in the practice simply because others do, and for them not to do so would place them at a severe comparative disadvantage. The Federal Reserve Bank of Chicago reported that many areas do so because, "despite the risks, the competitive nature of the economic development game prevents them from exercising unilateral restraint; to do so invites economic decay."[25] As a result, many communities may be engaging in the practice without really wanting to do so. Leaders in states and localities must exercise supreme caution in competing in this way. Not all situations have worked out as was expected.

One of the problems with the use of incentives to date has had to do with contractual provisions for demonstrated results over time and the "clawback" of funds from companies that did not meet those obligations. Such performance-based incentive agreements contractually protect communities with agreed-upon reactions if forecasted job creation or investment goals are not met. This requires communities to treat these agreements as they would any other legal contract. Bartik notes that "local policy makers can include clawback provisions to recover some of the subsidy if the firm leaves too soon...Clawback provisions in economic development subsidies have been upheld by the courts, but only if such provisions are in writing and are explicit about the company's obligations."[26] "Clawbacks comprising repayment and penalties insert an inherent cost of money to the private company receiving the incentives. If interest and penalties are not assessed when performance measures are not met, and the recipient is required only to repay the grant, and there is no cost to the company for the use of the incentive dollars over the years the monies were in use."[27] Thus, most such arrangements now carry interest penalties as part of the payback.

Perhaps the greatest of problems that have arisen from the use of incentives has been the actual cost of the revenues that were sacrificed in the original agreement. There have even been cases reported in which communities were so desperate for job growth that they have knowingly entered into agreements in which they knew, up front, that they would give up more than they could ever gain, or that the returns would not be realized for decades.

Some incentive programs have been employed that have worked. There are also some arguments in favor of the use of business attraction incentives. The former governor of Kentucky, Paul Patton, described his state as a place companies bypassed. And, he maintains, without enough challenging jobs, the most skilled in the workforce were leaving the state in search of greater opportunities. He cites Ford and the Lexmar Corporation as two examples of successful uses of economic development incentives. Although they were two companies that were hardly in need of financial assistance, Patton maintained that the incentives were wise in the long run because they did create a lot of jobs.[28]

However, one must consider whether even desperately needed jobs are worth the incentives provided. Should a community pay $8,000 for a job thereby created? How about $50,000 per job? Some actual costs are shown in Table 2.1.

Finally, policy makers must be aware of several treacherous issues involved in the use of economic development incentives. The first is the problem of establishing a precedent. If company A receives an incentive package, how does one decline to grant company B a similar benefit? If the locality is willing to sacrifice tax revenues to *attract* company C to the community, how does it respond when company D applies for similar benefits to *remain* in the community? What do officials tell their existing businesses, who continue to pay taxes, when their payments

Table 2.1   Major Automakers' Location Incentive Packages

Company	State	Total Incentive Package (est.)	Cost Per Job (est.)
Nissan	Tennessee	$ 33 million +	$ 8,000
Mazda	Michigan	$ 49 million +	$14,000
Saturn	Tennessee	$ 70 million	$23,000
Diamond Star	Illinois	$118 million	$40,700
Toyota	Kentucky	$150 million	$50,000

Source: Jeffrey A. Finkle. "Location Incentives are Unfair and Poorly Justified." *GeoFax*, Conway Data. March 23, 2009.

are, in effect, paying for the tax base to which the newcomers are being excused from contributing? Can one make the same argument to the tax-paying residents of the community?

Another pitfall that policy makers must take pains to avoid is any use of incentives for purely political purposes. Bartik explains the political problem: "A ribbon-cutting at a new plant or plant expansion attracts attention. Providing a tax break allows a governor or a mayor to take credit for good news. Much of the cost of this tax break may be deferred to the future."[29]

For the purpose of this book, suffice it to conclude that incentives, if used at all, must be reflected in very tight contracts that protect the interests of the community, and must be very well-conceived, thoroughly explained, and clearly connected to the overall financial planning for, and economic growth of, the community.

2.5.3 Exercising the Right of Eminent Domain

The expected benefits of community uses of the right of eminent domain have to be tempered with the political and individual costs. Traditional use of this right was on the basis of resolving the problems of blighted areas or to make way for projects that significantly advanced the public's interests. The traditional basis for its application has been the constitutionally guaranteed (Fifth Amendment) right to be justly compensated for the public taking of personal property.

In 2005, the U.S. Supreme Court ruled in the Connecticut case of *Kelo v. New London*. In this ruling, the court narrowly decided that localities may exercise this right in the cause of job creation and the general furtherance of local economic development objectives. The *Kelo* decision effectively grants local officials, whom they felt were the best able to make decisions in support of the collective well-being, broad powers to decide when the taking of private property lies within the public's interest because such action will permit the expansion of the local job base. As reported in Garrett and Rothstein, thirty states subsequently acted to limit the powers of the public in this regard, either through legislation or constitutional amendments.[30] Justice Sandra Day O'Connor expressed the minority opinion that the Court has opened up the possibility of localities deciding that it is alright to replace a Motel 6 with a Ritz Carlton, or a farm with a factory, because they employ more people.[31]

The Court's decision and the immediate reactions to it have raised both the awareness and the public scrutiny of any efforts to exercise this right. This does not, however, mean that there will be no instances in which a community should not use this power in the best interests of the public. It is clear that there are situations in which allowing purely market forces to provide the best sites for facilities or infrastructure will not always result in the best locations being used. Indeed, one might imagine a situation in which a limited amount of land is available that will suit an employers' several location criteria. Although the public taking of land and property in exchange for fair market value must certainly be used with extreme caution, it is a power that some communities may need to attract employers and that should not be discounted out-of-hand.

Curt Pringle, former mayor of Anaheim, California, is an outspoken opponent to the local use of eminent domain. Pringle stated that local officials should put more effort into how to accomplish their planning goals without relying on this eminent domain. If they did, he asserts, "they'd find that urban development could occur without eminent domain...If local officials regularly made zoning requirements more flexible and acknowledged market principles, new projects could move forward without taking away from existing landowners."[32]

The question for local elected officials, then, must be one of balance. But balance is really the second issue that needs to be considered. First, the community must assure itself that there are no other possible solutions that are adequate. If, however, other sites are not acceptable to the prospective employer, and the community runs the risk of losing a major economic development prospect, then the local leadership must confront the issue of balance. The decision will then center around the costs—monetary, political, and otherwise—of falling back on eminent domain to ensure that all such costs do not exceed the long-term benefits to the community as a whole.

While communities may support or, at least tolerate, the use of this power once or even twice, there will be a limited number of times that officials will be permitted to do so. This proscribes that communities elect to do so only in the most extreme and potentially rewarding situations. It also means that elected officials who believe that there are several areas within the jurisdiction that are potential for this exercise may wish to address more than one such situation together and not have to make several attempts over time.

Eminent domain is a tool to be used sparingly. There are numerous examples of its prudent and proper application. Eminent domain served the local officials in Brea, California, as an "important tool in preparing the downtown for redevelopment. In negotiations, the threat of eminent domain prevented the few property owners that would ask for selling prices significantly above fair market value from stalling the process."[33] There have been many situations in which eminent domain has been well and properly used. A situation in which the elected leadership of a community will ultimately decide to use this power will be one of those times when decision makers may believe that the community's best economic interests outweigh not only the costs to individuals, but the political costs to themselves as well. Obviously, it is a power to wield judiciously.

2.5.4 Communicating Success

Success in enhancing local economic growth can beget even greater success. Business locations acquire recognition as good places in which to operate either a specific type of business or for businesses in general. This awareness is invaluable as it aids in the attraction of additional employers as well as in the retention of existing employers as they grow. But the reality of being a good business location must be matched by the perceptions of business decision makers.

Communities pursuing further economic growth must take aggressive and constant steps to advise the target industry sectors of their interest in supporting economic growth and the assets and amenities they possess that will be of benefit to businesses. A well-rounded program of communications that incorporates advertising, public relations, special events, and more will deliver the message. The keys are constancy, consistency, using multiple vehicles to reinforce the messages, and repetition over long periods of time.

2.6 Emerging Directions for Community Growth

A variety of new concepts have arisen in recent years to facilitate local economic growth. They purport to do so by establishing in one community or one neighborhood what amounts to a competitive advantage to locate a facility there rather than elsewhere.

Town centers that possess the charms of a city environment in a suburban location have sprung up to provide alternatives to more traditional suburban neighborhoods. These town centers—like Reston Town Center near Washington-Dulles International Airport in northern Virginia—possess the higher densities and mixed uses more typically found in city locations.

Businesses have found these to be attractive locations. Reston Town Center has now grown to a residential population of more than 7,000 and an office space inventory that is approaching five million square feet, accommodating about 19,000 workers.[34] One of the selling points for businesses to locate in town centers is the closer proximity to their workforce. This translates into reduced travel, reduced tardiness, and minimized environmental impacts.

A variety of federal and state programs have grown that allow tax incentives to locate in distressed areas. Once again, these are efforts designed to distinguish one area over another and to give it a competitive disadvantage. In these programs, the intent is generally to encourage greater consideration by businesses of the areas in greatest need. Of course, businesses will more naturally be inclined to select locations in the more upscale markets where other businesses have located. This raises the question of what communities can do to entice businesses to consider submarkets other than just the most desirable locations in their communities.

Communities have endorsed a number of programs designed to make real differences while creating an impression on the part of site location consultants and decision makers that a given location is more "livable" or more "green" or "cooler." These images are the result of actions taken to make the community more supportive of environmentally friendly policies or more open to cultural opportunities and the arts.

The "Cool Cities" program, for example, seeks to reverse municipal activities contributing to global warming and sets as its goal "to reduce global warming carbon dioxide pollution in their cities to 7% below 1990 levels by 2012." Four hundred U.S. mayors, representing 61 million Americans, have signed on ("Cool Cities," http://www.SierraClub.org, March, 2007). Such programs not only make real change, but help brand communities as forward-thinking, thereby attracting the attention of businesses that have similar attitudes and concerns.

There is a great deal of literature about the importance of communities being more open and creative as those actions and that reputation will help attract the creative companies and creative individuals that will generate the economic growth of tomorrow. This will be covered in greater length later as the recent work of Richard Florida and others will be examined.

2.7 Viewing Local Economic Growth from Different Perspectives

2.7.1 Elected Officials

For the elected officials of a community, economic growth serves a clear primary purpose: the provision of employment and income stability, and the quality and quantity of public services that constitute the quality of life they were elected to ensure and enhance.

Economic growth means not only a secure job base and the income to obtain what one needs in life. It also translates into enhanced tax revenues that enable localities to provide for quality public education, police and fire protection, various public works, parks, libraries, and more. Local elected officials bear the responsibility for providing such services with the highest level of quality possible given the resources available. Growth of the local business base means the addition of resources to get the job done. And, given the resultant and relatively lesser demand for public services from the business community, such growth can permit the provision of services and an enhanced quality of life while minimizing the burden of those costs on residents. Typically, it is acknowledged that, when a business pays a tax dollar, it receives, in turn, far less than a dollar in public services. On the other hand, residents receive collectively much more value in public services than they contribute to the local tax base. This is, in large measure, due to the costs to local government of providing a public education system.

Clearly, there is a balancing act to be performed by local elected officials. Economic growth can translate into enhanced job security and wealth generation for constituents as well as enhanced business services without overtaxing residents. It generates new customers for existing businesses as well as a general trickle-down effect as more dollars are spent and re-spent in the local economy.

But the benefits of local economic growth can, to some extent, be offset by the resultant consequences: increased traffic and other congestion, environmental impacts, the rising costs and availability of housing, and more. Mayors and council and board members are charged with making these balancing decisions. It is virtually a guarantee that, whether decisions are made to pursue growth or to resist it, a fair percentage of the constituency will be in favor, some will be in opposition, and the balance will fall in between, perhaps taking a "wait and see" attitude. It is very important that the local economic development strategic plan anticipate and be responsive to these kinds of concerns. The concluding chapter of this book will address the ways in which community leaders can help residents understand and embrace the decisions to pursue economic growth locally.

These decisions may not always be based in purely economic or employment terms. In Fairfax County, Virginia, in the late 1970s and early 1980s, the Board of Supervisors supported a dramatically greater level of effort from its economic development program, in part, for the kinds of practical reasons already noted. But there was also an emotional reason: families benefited from the existence of arguably the finest public education system in the United States and sent their children to some of America's finest colleges and universities. In that time period, however, initiating their careers meant relocation to California, New York, Boston, or elsewhere. Economic development meant that children could come home to start their careers and families could stay together.

Although such emotional points as a job base to which children could return are somewhat qualitative, there can be factors that are quantifiable as well. But not all benefits are measurable and not all benefits are evident to residents. An enhanced business base in a community means support—both financial and other—for community-based organizations. Many companies may be thought of as good corporate citizens who contribute to programs for arts and culture, youth programs, the indigent, medical research, and more. These can become strong selling points for the elected official who wants to encourage support for his or her decision to pursue economic growth in the community. Conversely, an economic downturn typically causes businesses to curtail their community and charitable contributions and sponsorships as the first means of balancing their own tight budgets.

2.7.2 Practitioners

In this case, the term *practitioner* is understood to mean those who influence and manage the growth processes of a community. This will include economic development representatives—both professional and advisory—as well as land use, zoning, and permitting professionals and other staff and officials of the municipality or region whose responsibilities can either hinder or facilitate local economic growth.

To a very large extent, practitioners are the tools of the elected body. Although they may play an important role in promulgating and determining the local growth policy, ultimately it is their role to carry out the vision set forth by those who are elected to set the plans for a community's future. When regarded this way, the process can be boiled down to translating the established vision into operating plans and striving to accomplish the stated objectives in the most effective and efficient manner possible, given the levels of capital and human resources available.

The perspective of the economic development professional, then, should be abundantly clear. Success is not always a given, despite the finest of plans, due to changes in the environment and, as has already been discussed, the highly competitive nature of the function. For an economic development professional, a relocation decision that favors another community is quite simply a loss! This is even more emphatically clear in some areas. For example, in the Commonwealth of Virginia, local governments do not have authorization to impose a local income tax. Resources from which Virginia's local governments provide public services for their constituents come largely from the real estate tax base. In Fairfax County, nearly two-thirds of General Fund expenditures come from its real estate tax base. This means that the Fairfax County Board of Supervisors funds its Economic Development Authority to increase the tax base, thus reducing the burden of public service costs for residents. This is done by filling existing office space and generating a demand for the new construction that adds to the tax base. In this scenario, nearby business growth does not constitute a "win."

Practitioners in other states may regard proximate business growth differently. Even if it is not within their immediate borders, the growth of businesses will provide jobs for their constituents and contracting opportunities for the small businesses in the area. Again, the perspectives of the local economic development professionals will tie directly back to the vision and growth strategies set by the local elected officials, as well as the environmental context in which they operate.

2.7.3 The Residential Community

The perspective of the residents of a community is extraordinarily difficult to capture in text because there are many different individual contexts. The existing resident who needs a job or who can qualify for a higher wage in one of the new businesses in town will likely be supportive, whereas those who already possess job security and are not in need of additional wealth or services may be less supportive of growth in the community. To the extent that residents own land, new residents who come to work for new employers in a community will benefit from demand-driven increases in property values. Those wanting to buy may need to save longer.

In short, there are lots of residential situations and individual sets of circumstances that can generate opinions about growth in the community. Of course, not everyone can be categorized so easily. There will be some who, despite their own security, will recognize the need for the community to grow. And, there will be some who, despite their own particular needs, may oppose growth on the grounds that the impacts on the existing quality of life are simply not worth it. Quality-of-life factors will always be important to the community. Roy Lubove wrote that "a region's quality of life and basic livability are particularly important for service-based businesses of all kinds. Enhancing Pittsburgh's image in this regard can be particularly helpful to firms as they compete to retain or attract engineering and other technical talent."[35] Regardless of the differing points of view of the residents in a community, the elected officials will need to coalesce all of the stakeholders to create the communitywide spirit and effort required to be successful in economic development.

2.7.4 The Business Community

Although one might expect all business people to be generally supportive of economic growth, it is important not to oversimplify their perspective. Businesses are comprised of individuals, some of whom will be concerned about congestion and environmental impacts just like anyone else. There will even be situations in which one or more businesses will be concerned about the attraction of new employers to an area if they regard them as competitors. Conversely, some employers will view the attraction of competitors as a positive direction if it contributes to the evolution of specific business clusters and the benefits they bring to all.

Generally speaking, however, business people can be expected to recognize the benefits of growth and to understand the need for growth at the local and regional levels. Indeed, their support in the process is vital. Economic development is not the domain simply of government officials. This may be especially true in regional settings because businesses are less likely to be parochial about where jurisdictional boundaries lie. Further, business people can play critical roles in the economic development process: they can help identify prospects, help market the community, share experiences with prospects considering a given location, and provide invaluable insights and guidance to the local economic development staff. It has been evident in one economic development prospect situation after another that the businesses being courted expect local officials to be positive about the benefits of doing business in their community. It is a different matter entirely to hear directly from a peer about the strengths and weaknesses of one community relative to another.

Additionally, business people tend to regard the enhanced health and sustainability of the local economy as important. That is why there are chambers of commerce and business and professional associations. From this perspective will come some extremely valuable allies in the process of ensuring sustainable growth in communities and regions.

For businesses considering an area as a potential site for a new facility or considering remaining in a community, local government practices become important considerations. This is true not only in terms of the quantity and quality of public services they receive and the value they place on those services relative to the taxes they pay. Businesses are also greatly attuned to the regulatory environment of the states and localities in which they operate. Businesses do not generally argue that there should be no regulations; they do maintain, however, that regulations should be constructive and protective of all. Further, there is an expectation that regulations that are imposed will be fair, consistent from one application to another, and consistent over time. Business leaders also frequently object to the proscription of *how* to accomplish mandated goals. An oft-cited preference is to state the objectives of various requirements and allow the businesses to determine how best to accomplish them.

An additional frustration often heard from businesses engaged in the relocation, permitting, or zoning processes of a community relates to the numerous points of entry they typically encounter and the time frames required to negotiate these processes. Localities that wish to be considered business-friendly and that wish to enhance their economic bases need to review these processes to ensure that they are as expeditious as possible without sacrificing safety or ignoring other vital public requirements. Local administrators can also improve the reputation of their communities by providing a single point of entry and an "account executive" who will marshal their plans through all the necessary processes and provide counsel along the way.

A mistake that too many communities make is to devote great resources to the attraction of new businesses to the exclusion of efforts to retain those that are already present in the area. Certainly, one can agree that relocation to a locality also implies relocation *from* another area. The obverse of the same set of factors that attract businesses to a community will send them away from their existing locations. The absence of proximity to markets or suppliers, the need for infrastructure or a better quality of life, and quality measures of the public education system can either be strong lures or powerful deterrents.

Communities must recognize, as do the businesses themselves, that a repeat customer is the greatest source of stability over time. Business people will also acknowledge that happy customers are important not only because they return (or, stay in town), but also because they will relate their satisfaction in doing business in a location to their colleagues. In this way, they can become the greatest advocates for further economic growth in an area. However, business people will also tell you that a disgruntled customer is far more likely to spread the negative word than is a satisfied customer to spread positive stories. Thus communities, like businesses, need to keep in close contact with their existing businesses to ensure that they stay in place as they grow and contribute to the economy.

It behooves community leaders to stay in touch with local business executives not only so they will stay in place, but also to gain advance knowledge of decisions to leave. Although this is clearly not the desired outcome, it does happen in every community as times and needs change. It is certainly advantageous in these situations for communities to be made aware of such negative dispositions of site location decision-making processes. It allows the community to handle damage control and to work on public statements with the company's executives. If a business leaves town due to uncontrollable factors, it is vital that the news be characterized that way. Otherwise, there is room left for business executives to reach false conclusions about why a company is leaving a given location. Such false conclusions can affect a community's general reputation as a good place to conduct business operations.

Another interesting cause of the need to conduct business retention programs may best be classified under the heading "no good deed goes unpunished." Communities that have been successful over time in growing their local economies create an attractive target for other communities to visit their companies and encourage them to consider their communities as good business location alternatives. Thus, it is the more successful localities that most need to work hard to hold on to what they've got.

2.8 Planning for Local Economic Growth

Communities can no longer simply rely on economic growth to come to them. They must be aggressive and consistent in their pursuit of the business development that leads to general, sustainable economic growth. And once it has been acquired, communities cannot take the continuation of such growth for granted. Strategic planning concepts have been successfully applied for much longer by the private sector than the public sector. Economic development strategic plans must be well thought out and must have the highest level of support possible in the community. Strategic planning can accelerate the process of local economic growth by establishing a focus on the most productive areas to pursue.

"Strategic planning is a process by which an organization attempts to control its destiny rather than allowing future events to do so. By appraising future opportunities and its own existing and future strengths and weaknesses, an organization can help ensure its success and avoid identifiable problems. Following the lead of the business community, local governments have come to embrace the concept of strategic planning."[36]

Of course, different communities have different needs. Thus, the process of strategic planning, although comprised of similar processes from one location to the next, will differ according to the relevant needs of the community. "Many communities have…recognized the value of strategic planning in the same way that companies have. One small town, which initiated an ambitious planning process, indicated it needed the process to do the following:

- Provide a plausible interpretation of the future and a sense of direction and enthusiasm;
- Foster cooperation and consistency between actions taken by public, private, and educational sectors;
- Prioritize initiatives which have wide community support;
- Make better use of community support; and
- Ensure government is appropriately organized to respond to priorities."[37]

This reference to the process of strategic planning for communities is a critical one. "To fully appreciate the benefits of strategic planning, it is useful to recognize its nature: it is both a *process* and a *product*. The process involves a systematic examination of the organization and its environment by those who have a stake in its future success. The product is a document specifying the actions required to achieve future goals based on the information unearthed during the planning process. Together, these components of strategic planning yield numerous benefits to any organization."[38]

The optimal approach to the strategic planning process involves the evolution of a community state of mind. "The creation of a strategic mind-set is vital in the strategic planning process. There must evolve a type of strategic thinking that is directed from the very top of the local government organization and that focuses constantly on issues affecting the future of the locality and the ability of its government to be successful. Strategic thinking in a community generally evolves with the strategic planning process over the years. Organizations whose strategic planning processes are in an early stage of development tend to be oriented to 'number crunching.' As the planning process evolves, changes occur: the planning increasingly focuses on issues instead of numbers and the members of the organization accept and comply with the planning process and the plan itself. Perhaps most importantly, the roles of the senior managers of the organization change."[39]

In the long run, the strategic planning process of any community will begin with the inherent beliefs of the key stakeholders. These beliefs comprise the general approach the involved players of the area take when discussing vital matters. Indeed, these beliefs are so important that they are often itemized in the plans of communities as background information for the reader. "The elements of the underlying beliefs of an organization have to been summarized in various ways." One such classification includes

- attitudes toward change;
- degree of consensus between senior officials;
- standards and values;
- concern for people;
- attitudes toward openness and communication;
- conflict resolution style (i.e., win/lose versus win/win);
- group orientation toward the market, the consumer;
- excitement, pride, *esprit de corps*;
- commitment; and
- teamwork."[40]

The economic growth of a community does not just happen. It requires leadership, structure, and process. But neither does strategic planning just happen. It, too, requires leadership, structure, process, and the consistent and collaborative involvement of the community's key stakeholders.

2.9 Concluding Thoughts

For communities that want to grow, there are several models based on various theoretical foundations to employ. There is also a plethora of tools that can be used, any of which can be used either to advantage or with less constructive outcomes.

The overriding concern must be for communities to pursue well-planned courses of action that have their bases in a broad consensus and the coordination of the various forms of communitywide planning.

Such planning is more critical for localities today than ever before. Change is more rapid, more far-reaching, and more all-encompassing than in the past, and it is more clearly driven by economic growth and contraction at the local level. This is why a static economic environment is unlikely: communities are either growing or in relative decline.

Society's increased mobility also means that communities must compete more than in the past for economic growth. The theoretical foundations that help explain why some places thrive while others decline must therefore also change. As such, local leaders in governments and business, as well as constituents, will regard economic growth through different and changing lenses. Once again, the requisite changes in decisions about local structure and process require planning, foresight, coordination, and balance. In this practice, there are both "do" and "don't" examples. The next chapter considers some of the latter cases.

Notes

1. Hevesi, "Smart Growth in New York State: A Discussion Paper," 4.
2. Bernard and Rice, *Sunbelt Cities,* 200.
3. Hevesi, "Smart Growth," 13. What is unclear is the extent to which communities in other states fall into the same category as those of New York where, according to Hevesi, many have master land use plans that must be considered out of date. Given the pace of change, however, and the many challenges that confront growth communities in this age, it is entirely possible that the same statement could be applied around the United States.
4. "Development without Eminent Domain," http://www.castlecoalition.org/pdf/publications/perspectives-pringle.
5. Puget Sound Regional Council, "Populations of Cities and Towns."
6. Jacobs, *Great American Cities,* 418.
7. Stimson, Stough, and Roberts, *Regional Economic Development,* 25.
8. Bingham and Mier, *Theories of Economic Development,* 3.
9. Ibid., 3.
10. Shaffer, *Community Economics,* 26.
11. Ibid., 142.
12. Stimson, Stough, and Roberts, *Regional Economic Development,* 54.
13. Shaffer, *Community Economics,* 148.
14. Bingham and Mier, *Theories of Economic Development,* 29.
15. Bradbury, Kodrzycki, and Tannenwald, "The Effects of State and Local Public Policies on Economic Development: An Overview," 2.
16. Plosila, "Building Innovation-Driven Regional Economies in Small and Mid-Sized Metro Centers," *Economic Development America.* Washington D.C.: United States Department of Commerce, EDA, 2005, 5.

17. Downs, *New Visions,* 102.
18. Ibid., 90.
19. Bingham and Mier, *Theories of Economic Development,* 11. This is a critical point that is frequently made by site location professionals and consultants. Businesses seek locations where the political support is both apparent and consistent. Assurances are often sought that such support, including regulatory policies, taxes, and more, will remain constant over time and through the course of subsequent state and local elected administrations. States and localities that can demonstrate a longer term of pro-business actions and rhetoric have a significant advantage when attempting to attract and retain employers.
20. National Education Association. "School Funding Taxes, and Economic Growth," Washington, D.C., 2004, 6–7.
21. Lynch, *Arts and Economic Prosperity,* 9.
22. Downs, *New Visions,* 120.
23. Vedder, "State and Local Taxes and Economic Growth," 1.
24. Peters and Fisher, "The Failures of Economic Development Incentives," 28.
25. Federal Reserve Bank of Chicago, Challenges and Opportunities Ahead, 51. The argument that communities are often forced into offering location incentives, to remain competitive with other communities that do so, is an oft-heard claim. And indeed, in many instances, to be out of the incentives business does mean that prospects will not consider the locational opportunities in a given community. The consideration, however, is not entirely that cut-and-dried. Site location decision making is a highly refined art that incorporates an extensive and exhaustive series of factors including geographic factors, initial and long-term costs, labor pool, community resources, quality of life, and more. Incentives can realistically be seen as just one additional consideration that, if all other things are equal, may sway the decision.
26. Bartik, *Economic Development Policies,* 18.
27. Richmond, "Clawbacks in Economic Development: Policies and Practices," 1.
28. Patton, "Development Incentives Are a Win–Win Proposition for Companies, Communities," 1.
29. Bartik, "Jobs, Productivity, and Local Economic Development: What Implications Does Economic Research Have for the Role of Local Government?," 848.
30. "The Taking of Property: *Kelo v. New London* and the Economics of Eminent Domain," http://www.stlouisfed.org/publications/re/2007/a/pages/prosperity.html.
31. Ibid.
32. "Development without Eminent Domain," www.castlecoalition.org/pdf/publications/Perspectives-Pringle, 3.
33. "Eminent Domain Resource Kit," International Economic Development Council, 12.
34. Fairfax County Economic Development Authority.
35. Lubove, *Twentieth Century Pittsburgh,* 130.
36. Gordon, *Strategic Planning Local Government,* 1.
37. Ibid., 2.
38. Ibid., 3–4.
39. Ibid., 61.
40. Ibid., 22.

Chapter 3

Local Economies in Decline: How to Lose the Business Base

3.1 Introduction

Economic decline is usually associated with communities experiencing job loss or a slowing of productivity for various reasons and, as a result, suffering the worst of several sociocultural problems that are attendant to the absence of opportunity or hope. These include higher crime rates, the loss of the best of the labor force, the loss of the families that can afford to depart for more prosperous climes, and the loss of the tax base. What is left is a labor pool with generally lower skill levels, less education and experience, and less drive.

Shaffer describes community reactions to the loss of economic stability in the same way that individuals react to personal loss: through the successive stages of denial, anger and blame, depression and withdrawal, and finally, acceptance and hope. In the initial phase—denial—Shaffer maintains that community leaders may believe that "things will work out." Disruptions in the local economy may, in this phase, be regarded as temporary or cyclical, not motivating the local leadership into any formal response. Thus, the underlying causes of the decline may go unexamined. Shaffer further suggests that the anger/blame phase is characterized by "finger-pointing" as local officials may look for those who are at fault for allowing the problem to occur rather than seeking to correct the underlying causes. In the ensuing stage of depression and withdrawal, communities may stagnate and remain inactive. It is only after the community accepts the situation that it is typically motivated to respond, plan, react, and begin to recover.[1]

It is clear that economic decline in communities creates a spiraling effect that contributes to the deterioration of the very conditions that would enable them to reverse their fortunes. As Bartik explains, local governments cannot simply make proportionate budget cuts to offset the losses. "Local economic decline will tend to lead to a…decline in public revenues. But, infrastructure costs will not decline. The infrastructure is already in place and has in part already been financed. It is usually infeasible to abandon much existing infrastructure, and this would only save maintenance costs."[2] Bates is even more direct: "The resources that might enable a depressed area to break out of its downward trajectory are precisely the resources that are prone to drain out."[3]

This describes a poor setting for business attraction and one in which jobs and the collective expendable income actually decline over time. And yet, some of America's greatest centers of business of the past are in decline today. Bates specifically cites Detroit; Gary, Indiana; and various cities in upstate New York as examples. "All suffer from a slow, long-term loss of competitive position. Leading firms in these regions—Ford, U.S. Steel, Kodak, Xerox, and others—previously enjoyed powerful oligopolistic positions in their respective industries."[4] And the communities in which they were located believed that they had a firm grasp on long-term economic stability. And all of that changed; and rather rapidly at that.

These situations will be discussed in later chapters. They are in stark contrast to communities that, in an attempt to control or stop growth, can inadvertently drive the local economy into a spiral of decline. And, as Downs points out, growth management policies "often limit annual additions to the supply of various types of property in the adopting community. This slows the pace of development and inevitably diverts potential new development to other localities nearby."[5] What is left are the least desirable development opportunities. Loveridge describes what happens: "In declining regions…people are concerned about eroding property values, loss of youth, declining local government tax base, and reduced availability of services such as local schools, hospitals, or restaurants…Declining regions are typically more willing to receive activities that bring with them a high level of negative externalities. Low wage jobs, prisons, and landfills become attractive options for economic developers working in a region facing long-term economic decline…A short-term focus is a likely outcome of this situation."[6]

Although the impacts may be different in the initial phases, the same issues can be observed. Is slowing or stopping growth really such a good idea?

3.2 The Consequences of No-Growth Policies: Jobs, the Tax Base, and Economic Stagnation

The economic fortunes of some communities decline as the result of outside factors, that is, forces over which there is little or no local control. These factors may include global or national recession, unexpected losses of industries or primary employers, or a host of other factors. In the context of the environment present at the writing of this book, it is a self-evident fact that local economies can decline due to uncontrollable factors. The banking crisis, a wildly falling stock market, the housing and subprime mortgage debacles, and the demise of corporate giants have all conspired to create ripples that are washing over states, regions, and localities throughout the nation and around the world.

Clearly, local leadership does not have the ability to control these matters or even to exert much control over the aftershocks they are creating. The lesson that can be gleaned from this experience is one that has been cited and that will be mentioned several times over in this book. Local governments must establish the foundations of a strong economic base during the good economic times so it and its residents can better sustain it during the bad times. To wait until the situation is dire is to create too many obstacles to being successful when the needs are critical.

Of course, there are a variety of factors in local economic growth that, at least to some extent, are within the control of local officials. These include land use decisions, tax policies, the quality of public education or other public services, or policies specifically aimed at controlling the growth of the local economy.

The Smart Growth Network of New York State notes that "various ideas advanced under the rubric of smart growth cover a wide spectrum, ranging from rehabilitation of city, town, and village centers while strictly limiting peripheral growth, to supporting any growth where the value of more development is perceived to outweigh potential negative effects."[7]

A number of titles have been attached to policies that are intended solely to impede growth. Slow growth and no growth, as examples, are somewhat clear in their meanings. Other monikers, however, can be more elusive and used to cover a wide range of sentiments and a host of actual intentions. Planned growth is an oft-used term that, on the surface, implies that growth will continue, but in a carefully designed manner. In practice, planned growth has sometimes served as a cover for slow or no-growth when its architects wished to appear in less than total opposition to growth for political or other reasons.

The term of art that has been the most elusive to describe accurately has been "smart growth." Its elusiveness derives from the fact that "smart" is in the eye of the beholder. Whereas one person might think of smart growth as slower or faster, another might think of it simply as being more orderly; for example, development that follows the provision of adequate infrastructure to support the growth. Some, reported Sunnucks (*Washington Business Journal*, August 18, 2000), have even equated smart growth with "an intrusion upon private property rights."

And Hevesi adds that "a major criticism of smart growth is that it seeks to substitute a certain set of judgments for the natural products of free enterprise and local control, which ultimately reflects the choices of citizens with regard to where and how they live, work, and travel."[8] Often, it is simply a mask for those who are completely anti-growth, but realize that such a characterization will not be as effective politically. After all, who can argue with being smart about growth or anything else? As Hevesi wrote, "it is hard to argue with the core idea of smart growth—that there are connections between development patterns and our quality of life, economy, and environment, and that growth should improve rather than harm our communities."[9] The Sunnucks piece (*Washington Business Journal*, August 18, 2000) takes measure of that perspective by quoting a representative of the Maryland Chamber of Commerce: smart growth could "quickly become a code phrase for anti-business, regulations and taxes. That could hurt the state's efforts, especially with the proximity of pro-business, right-to-work states such as Virginia and North Carolina."

A fair definition of smart growth is provided by Westmoreland County, Oregon. "Smart growth is development that serves the economy, the community, and the environment. It changes the terms of the development debate away from the traditional growth/no-growth question to 'how and where should new development be accommodated?' Smart growth answers these questions by simultaneously achieving healthy communities, economic development and jobs, and strong neighborhoods."[10]

But the impact of such policies can be overwhelmingly damaging to the community. Hevesi notes that the smart growth movement, in other words, is "premised on dissatisfaction with current development practices."[11] In the last decade of the twentieth century, the state of Oregon became synonymous with slow- and no-growth policies. The intention, as will be seen in the case study later in this book, was to slow growth through a variety of means, including limits on corporate job creation. The impacts of those policies on the city of Portland were so severe that many still have memories of the state as business-unfriendly.

Flint warns that local decision makers need to be careful when embracing smart growth programs because the goals of smart growth movements usually appear quite reasonable. However, when queried about the methods of accomplishing their objectives, the answers are often less clear and more questionable. He further maintains that every smart growth plan must be centered around transportation improvements. In the absence of enhanced transportation networks, for example, the calls for increased densities that characterize many smart growth outlines may only result in increased gridlock where the most people live and work. Only getting people out of their cars and walking or taking public transportation will allow truly smart growth to occur.[12]

O'Toole takes the arguments against smart growth as it is generally practiced today a step further by maintaining that such movements have the effects of increasing both suburban and urban densities, wasting funds on rail systems that relatively few people will actually ride, adopting automobile-hostile (as opposed to pedestrian-friendly) design codes, and creating regional governments that can foist policies on unwitting and reluctant suburban jurisdictions.[13]

Anthony Downs carries the debate to the social ills of American downtowns. "The most dangerous result of growth management policies is that they help perpetuate the concentration of very poor households in depressed neighborhoods in big cities and older suburbs…they are riddled with the most virulent forms of four problems that are undermining social cohesion and economic efficiency throughout the nation: exploding rates of crime and violence, increased numbers of children growing up in poverty, poor-quality public education, and failure to integrate workers into the mainstream workforce."[14]

The reality, however, is that smart growth movements adopt sets of principles and objectives that are unique to the area for which they are planned. In this context, smart growth advocates are most often serious and sincere about improving their communities through prior planning and rational decision making. These tend to be grassroots movements that have significant support in their communities. The key to rational smart growth must certainly be in the means as well as the ends. Local elected officials must ensure that the pursuit of their goals does not yield any unintended consequences for the long-term economic future of their communities. However, Hevesi cautions that "because growth occurs across municipal borders, many smart growth principles involve regional planning and solutions. These solutions may be difficult to achieve given the fragmented structure of land use, transportation, and economic development planning, as well as the tendency for local governments to compete for relative advantage."[15]

In this vein, Gillham cites the elements of most smart growth movements that, if applied in a balanced manner, can have significant impact on community planning. He includes "open space conservation; boundaries limiting the outward extension of growth; compact, mixed-use developments, amenable to walking and transit; revitalization of older downtowns, inner-ring suburbs, and run-down commercial areas; viable public transit to reduce auto dependence and support alternative development patterns; regional planning coordination (particularly of transportation and land use); and equitable sharing of fiscal resources and financial burdens, including affordable housing across metropolitan regions."[16]

Of course, there is no question that reasonable people, particularly those with strong leadership, can accomplish great things. However, it is when smart growth is used as a mask for no-growth or when the ends are pursued without regard for the means or for the long-term impacts on the economy that such movements can run afoul of the long-term best economic interests of the community. No-growth movements too often receive their impetus from land owners who are motivated by self-interest rather than the best long-term interests of the community. Of course, the same statement can too often be made about those who favor additional development. Determinations about the proper balance and the welfare of the community fall within the realm of the difficult choices that need to be made by constituents and their elected leadership. Later, case studies will consider some of these situations, the directions that were taken, and the ultimate results.

Zovanyi helps to explain how attitudes toward the sprawl that has spawned no-growth movements have changed over time. Initial reactions (in the 1960s and early 1970s) regarded regional expansion in terms of its positive attributes. It helped grow local economies and personal incomes while offering residents a variety of lifestyle choices. Over time, he asserts, attitudes changed as such expansions yielded the loss of agricultural areas and open space, congestion on the roads and in schools, and various environmental impacts. As a result, he cites a key distinction between growth management and no-growth efforts: growth management wishes not to stop growth, but to "make ongoing growth possible and acceptable."[17]

Clearly, growth can have significant benefits when managed well and for the right reasons and by applying the right tools for the particular setting. Growth can yield the tax revenues and other benefits that can help resolve other problems in communities. The undesirable consequences of growth must be addressed and, to the extent possible, resolved by community leadership, but it must be done with great caution lest the local economy stalls, leaving the problems to be addressed without the benefits growth can bring to a community. Local elected officials must be consistent and true to the test of what is best for their constituents. This means ignoring political expediency. There is a certain amount of truth in the statement that "land uses generally become highly politicized during economic boom periods, when pressure is placed on local housing and transportation resources; the political controversies usually die down during recessions, when economic development and jobs become the priority."[18]

3.3 Arresting Community Brain Drains

In the mid-1980s, elected officials in Fairfax County, Virginia, were still bemoaning the fact that children who grew up in the county and attended some of the best public schools in the United States and had in-state access to what are arguably some of America's finest public and private colleges and universities could not return to the community to start their careers unless they were interested in employment with the federal government. Those with an orientation to the private sector had to leave to find work. They either went to Boston or New York or California or elsewhere, but few returned home to start their careers.

A generation later, Fairfax County is home to more than six hundred thousand jobs, the vast majority of which are with private employers. Most importantly to the parents in the community, their children can come home to work, live, and raise their families. Most importantly for the businesses in the community, there is a steady supply of highly educated, skilled, and well-motivated young men and women who are ready to go to work for them.

What has become known as the "brain drain" from communities really represents a vicious cycle. These communities lose their most valuable asset for attracting businesses and creating new companies, which means that companies either leave or stay away. This, in turn, means that more of the youth have to leave the community for challenging employment opportunities, which results in companies staying away, and so on.

Given the array of financial and economic issues confronting America and its communities as this is being written, the issue of brain drains is perhaps even more relevant to some than ever before. Individuals and families must go where they are able to find employment opportunities. Those movements are being accelerated as the unemployment rates climb across the nation. This often leads communities to regret not having created a stronger job base during the good times that could sustain them through the more difficult economic times. Unfortunately, it is, by then, too late to create jobs in time to retain the very workforce that will be needed to attract new employers when the economic recovery begins.

The obvious question is how to avoid rather than arrest this problem. The answer must lie in becoming more competitive. The more that communities are able to establish the types of businesses that are appealing to skilled and educated workers, the more likely they will be to stop and even reverse the brain drain. In the absence of such a draw, the best and brightest will leave. George Raney, a resident of Fresno, California, summed it up very neatly in an interview. When the area's residents leave, he said, "it takes away from the culture and intellectual life of the valley." And the implications are not lost on the youth of this community. Reporter Maria La Ganga, (*Los Angeles Times,* November 20, 2005) surveyed the sophomore gifted English class in Fresno and learned that twenty-three of twenty-four intended to leave the community as soon as possible and that only one in four would ever even consider coming back at a later time. Without these young people, businesses will have little reason to be attracted to the community in the future.

Peaks and valleys in the economic fortunes of communities or regions can create periods of brain drain offset by periods of rapid growth in the employment base and intensive recruiting. Carlson, in a 2004 article (*San Jose Business Journal,* August 27, 2004), makes this point about the Silicon Valley: "A lot of people came out here in the boom and then went back where they came from when they lost their jobs in the late '90s…In the past, companies had to offer signing bonuses and forgivable loans for people to come out here and that might happen again."

A 2003 article in a publication of the American Agricultural Economics Association concludes that even for rural counties, "the brain drain is not an inherent problem…but something that might be overcome with properly designed, well-informed policies."[19] This affirms the notion that communities, urban or rural and large or small, can retain their best resource for future growth—its brain power—by implementing strategies to create a pro-business environment.

3.4 Community Gap Analyses

Communities that wish to reverse economic decline or the ill fortunes of impeded growth must evaluate themselves in terms of what they have to offer industry. Commerce in general has a base set of requirements. These include proximity to markets, a qualified and ample workforce from which to select, arrangements for training and retraining, the necessary infrastructure components to move both people and product, and a certain assumed quality of lifestyle. Given the very competitive nature of economic development, businesses are confronted daily with numerous options in which to locate their facilities. Communities can make no safe assumptions about their ability to receive companies without making proper efforts to attract them.

Neither can communities feel blindly confident that companies will remain in place. Business is business. If it can reduce its costs by being closer to their markets or by accessing lower rents or power or taxes, or better conditions, it will do so. Companies exist to enhance revenues and shareholder profits and they do so by increasing their effectiveness and efficiency, not by being supportive of a community in need despite the availability of better arrangements.

Superimposed over the listing of the general needs of commerce are the somewhat more specific requirements of given industries. Traditional manufacturers and high-tech manufacturers have different sets of requirements from a community in which they operate, as do data centers, software developers, or distributors. The third layer of asset analysis is for the specific company. No two companies, even those in the same industry segment, will have identical needs and interests. There are almost always discriminating factors that give one community an edge over others. Sometimes, it will not be quantifiable—or even identifiable. It may be a feeling of being more wanted in one community, or liking the physical site better, or even the natural beauty of the area.

The point is that the most successful pitch to business people from a community about location, retention, or expansion will be on the educated basis of his or her particular individual interests and needs. The community that understands those needs is halfway home to addressing them in specific terms rather than engaging in a general discussion about the area. The best way to ensure that the hot points are being addressed is to conduct as exhaustive research as is feasible on the industry, the company, and the individual decision makers before meeting with them.

Over time, this type of research will provide valuable intelligence about the needs and interests of businesses in general as well as businesses within specific industry segments. This will give rise to an overview of the community's strengths and weaknesses for attracting and retaining business. It will identify not only the characteristics that are in place to support economic growth, but what is missing as well. The missing elements represent the gap between the desire to grow and the ability. It is a road map for a community and its leadership to prepare the best setting for business. It is the means by which the economy will grow.

If businesses report that they have failed to select a location because the skill sets in the labor pool are not sufficient, training programs become a strategy and colleges or trade schools become strategic partners. Perhaps it's local regulations or tax policies. Maybe the issue is site and utility costs or distances to markets. Whatever the gaps identified, the local government will be left with a list of items to address if they wish to grow the economy, and attract either industry in general or specific industry segments.

A peripheral outcome of performing a community gap analysis can often be a cold splash of reality. Many communities, in the height of the dot.com explosion, wanted to get their share of high-tech start-ups and growth. Many approached the effort by changing their brands, and many attempted to "borrow" the Silicon Valley brand. The Silicon Valley had become a near-generic expression. When people thought of technology communities, they thought of the Silicon Valley in the same way that copiers make people think of Xerox or tissues make people think of Kleenex. Several years ago, I set about to discover how U.S. communities attempt to brand themselves. I searched 352 economic development Web sites throughout the United States. Interestingly, I discovered that exactly one hundred, or about 28 percent, had made an attempt to brand their communities, while the rest did not use a brand or tag line on their Web sites at all.

It is evident that some cities don't need to bother with branding exercises. Why does New York need to brand itself with anything? Everyone knows New York. They know where it is; they know what it is. However, for the city, the "Silicon Alley" was their effort to say, "Hey, we're New York, but we've got technology, too!" Of course, not all communities are as well-known as New York and feel a need to distinguish themselves from their (economic development) "competition" by branding themselves with a title that communicates either what they presently are, or what they wish to become. It got to the point that the competition to lay claim to being the Silicon Glen and the Silicon Fen and the Silicon Island and the Silicon (fill in the blank here) became fierce. Lawsuits were filed over communities rushing to be the first to claim credit as the Silicon Prairie.

Gap analyses would have forewarned many of those communities that there were gaps to attracting the technology community that could not be offset by a name change. Technology companies thrive where there are technology-trained and trainable workers, where there are training institutions that can provide workers and retraining and research and development support. They expect excellent public schools and a higher quality of life than the other communities that were in pursuit of their facilities. Attracting businesses is about knowing what companies want and providing the needed assets and resources, not in marketing what may or may not exist. Branding a community as a "Great Place to Grow" or "The Land of Opportunity" or "A State of Minds" may sound catchy, but companies will be attracted only by substance.

Gap analyses would have indicated clearly what communities' competitive strengths were and which to develop further. Alternatively, the results could have made clear that the necessary assets did already exist in their communities to attract and grow other industry or industry segments. Communities that aspire to attracting a business segment for which they do not have the right resources are missing one important lesson: businesses know very clearly what they need and whether or not a locality possesses those resources. If it does not, they will not locate there;

there will be no "talking them into" such decisions. Gap analyses indicate whether that success can be reasonably expected or not. In short, it can save a lot of time, energy, and goodwill.

Some communities have made the mistake of identifying the gap, but not moving sufficiently to close it. A publication of the U.S. Department of Labor Economic Development Administration notes that "successful regions don't just figure out what's missing. They put in place detailed implementation and investment plans at the operational level…to push actions and activities, but also to measure accountability." Such coalitions must "have a long-term commitment, and perseverance to catalyze and mobilize the private and public sectors to achieve concrete results."[20]

The intelligence that supports such gap analyses need not come just from businesses that leave or go elsewhere. It can also come from businesses that entered the community or who have decided to stay as they grow. What is important is why they did so and what needs to be increased or added to make them do so again in the future. It goes without saying that just identifying the gaps is only part of the effort; communities must approve policies that address their shortcomings. For now, however, we will turn to a case study of communities whose policies, while designed to control growth, actually had the effect of rejecting it.

3.5 Where Public Policies Have Contributed to Job Losses or Slower Job Growth

Consider the case of Portland, Oregon, a physically beautiful community whose leadership elected to forestall growth. The initial interest in growth control related to the expansion of the residential population, not commercial interests. O'Toole characterizes the Portland perspective as "the result of decades of efforts by Portlanders who wanted a strong regional government against suburbanites who valued their independence."[21]

Indeed, attempts to create regional government in Portland go back to the early 1900s. But, in 1992, Portlanders approved the creation of Metro, a seven-member council, serving more than 1.3 million residents and twenty-four cities, and that has the strongest regional land use and transportation planning powers of any metropolitan area in America. Based on the 1997 forecasts of dramatic population increases in the ensuing fifty years (80 percent), the council approved a series of policies to increase densities and expand public transportation links and required "city and county planners to rezone neighborhoods at higher densities to meet specific population targets so that new residents could be accommodated with minimal expansion of the urban growth boundary."[22]

In the late 1990s, officials in Oregon insisted that the state's largest private employer, Intel, include a highly unusual clause in the contract covering the state's investments to support the company's growth. One writer referred to it this way:

"Please don't create too many jobs!"[23] Intel thus received $200 million in property tax breaks in exchange for investments in equipment and facilities. The firm already employed more than four thousand people in its plant in the Portland area and would be permitted to increase that level by one thousand before incurring fines of $1,000 for each new employee put to work. A county spokesman was quoted as saying that "if Intel had been talking about 5,000 new jobs here, the sense is they wouldn't have gotten to first base."[24]

The growth boundaries have been effective in controlling population growth. Gillham reports that "nearly 90% of the state's population growth during the 1980s occurred inside UGB (Urban Growth Boundary) limits. In Portland, where the UGB includes Clackamas, Multnomah, and Washington Counties, and the city of Portland, it is estimated that 95% of population growth occurred within the UGB."[25] But, within the Portland UGB, commercial growth has not been equal. Gillham notes that, by the 1990s, downtown Portland was the site of 61 percent of the region's best office space inventory, but only 14 percent of its employment base. The urban sprawl had been kept from areas outside of the urban growth boundary, but had continued apace within. And, the core county, Multnomah, "lost 22,119 residents to other counties between 2000 and 2004."[26]

The UGB has, in many ways, been a success. Marshall states that "via the… Portland model, a center city can be re-pressurized, the energy of a region turned inward until the downtown streets begin to fill up again."[27] But, what impact has this planning approach had on businesses and the growth of the region's economy? And what other measures have been taken in Oregon that have impacted the ability of the state to grow either the state, regional, or local economies?

It became clear that, although the employment base grew in the outlying areas of the region, jobs in the downtown were not increasing. In 1993, the Oregon legislature enacted a Strategic Investment Program (SIP) that was designed to attract capital-intensive projects by limiting the property tax burdens. However, the SIP was amended to permit Washington County in suburban Portland to assess an impact fee on its largest employer, Intel. After four years of debate and consideration, the county reversed its position and opted to waive the requirements.

At the same time, the city of Portland and suburban Multnomah County exercised their rights to impose taxes on the net incomes of the venture capital companies located in those two jurisdictions. After this move generated local concerns about singling out one business sector for taxation, the policies were repealed. But this was done too late as those businesses had already moved out to neighboring jurisdictions. Clearly, the reviews of the UGB's performance have been mixed. Reporter Brian Back (*Portland Business Journal*, November 17, 2000) stated it this way: "To some, Portland's urban growth boundary is all that curbs the city from a future as just another megalopolis bedeviled by poorly planned subdivisions and seas of sedans and SUVs. To others, the UGB is a failed social experiment that limits citizens' right to their slice of the suburban pie and clogs a free-flowing, market-driven development economy."

Regardless of one's overall perspective, a clearly damaging legacy of the growth-control policies in Portland and Oregon is what Cortright and Mayer referred to as the area's "laid-back culture." They wrote that "to many, especially in the venture capital community, Portland seems hamstrung by its laid back culture; entrepreneurs seem less willing to sacrifice everything to grow the next Microsoft, and the community places little value on being wealthy and creating wealth."[28]

Public policies at both the state and local levels can have the effect of encouraging employers to depart for more business-friendly climes. To reverse these trends, local governments should focus on that which affects the business community and over which they exercise control: infrastructure, education, public safety, and taxes. But these same policy areas have also been used, either intentionally or unwittingly, to chase businesses away. Primary among these areas of potentially negative influence is the regulatory power of municipalities.

Porter argues that "more damaging than regulatory costs is the uncertainty that the regulatory process creates for potential investors." Managers who were interviewed by Professor Porter in Boston, Los Angeles, and Chicago expressed "frustration with the three-year to five-year waiting periods necessary to obtain the numerous permit and site approvals required to build, expand, or improve facilities. Undeniably, the wait is expensive; but the uncertainty about whether an application will be approved or when a ruling will be made makes forming a financial strategy nearly impossible."[29]

Still, the employment base in metropolitan Portland has grown. Between 1992 and 1997 alone, during the period of impact fees authorized under the Strategic Investment Plan, jobs grew from just under 650,000 to just over 800,000. However, it is quickly pointed out that a relatively small number of firms in a relatively few industrial segments accounted for a disproportionate share of the region's growth.[30]

Tim Priest, CEO of Portland's regional economic development organization, maintains that the people of Portland today feel vindicated for their decisions. And this claim has merit when one considers the many delegations that visit the region each year to learn how their areas can replicate the benefits of the Urban Growth Boundary plan and experience.

And, indeed, Portland is frequently cited as one of America's more "livable" cities. Priest points out, for example, that the region's emphasis on the preservation of green spaces has made it one of the country's most "bike-friendly" cities. This is not just a reference to recreational cycling, but also includes a relatively large proportion of residents who cycle to and from work.

Priest further asserts that quality-of-life considerations have been at the heart of all of Portland's decisions about growth. Residents believe that those decisions not only preserved the quality of life, but did so within the context of "managed, incremental growth," not no-growth. Although the Urban Growth Boundary has not always been flexible enough to respond immediately to all market forces, companies are easily able to attract a high-quality workforce to the region. "And, once they're here," states Priest, "they don't want to leave."[31]

An Internet-based report notes that the UGB has not been able to control growth completely either inside or outside of the borders, but hastens to add that "the lesson would not be that the Smart Growth efforts of Portland were wrong-headed, but that the best-thought plans cannot create a protective wall for nature that will withstand the continuous onslaught of population growth."[32]

Other examples of government policies that chased away jobs abound and they exist in a wide range of policy areas. Cohen and Garcia wrote, in the mid-1990s, that the factors that caused Los Angeles to lose as many as 56,000 jobs in the prior decade were obvious: "environmental regulations in the LA basin that simply shut down certain kinds of industrial processes; high overhead costs such as workers compensation which costs three times as much as in neighboring Oregon, or litigation costs that have risen by 300% on a per case basis over the past decade."[33]

In the 1990s, while marketing Fairfax County to businesses in the Los Angeles area, one businessman repeatedly told me of the additional tax burden placed on him by the state legislature because he owned the building in which his company was located. A requirement was set that would permit only a limited number of his employees to drive in to work and park in the lot at his building. The rule was based on the amount of square footage of office space his company owned and was intended to increase the use of public transportation. Soon, an official was stationed outside his building to count the number of cars, and he began to receive warning notices. These were followed by a series of monthly fines and, not long thereafter, his company's departure to the East Coast.

The state of Maine has also taken a variety of measures over the years that have left it with a reputation for approving regulations that chase businesses away from the state. In a 1990s effort to protect indigenous businesses in small Maine communities, several Maine towns enacted local ordinances that prohibited the existence of chain businesses. Often these retailers were among the largest employers in the town and often the greatest supporters of local little leagues, church and school activities, chambers of commerce, and other community organizations. And they departed.

In 2007, the state legislature authorized the Informed Growth Act (IGA). This legislation gives Maine's cities and towns the ability to evaluate the economic impacts of large-scale retail developments and to decline such growth if they believe it will have an adverse impact on jobs, local businesses, or municipal finances. The debate that preceded the passage of the legislation centered around which type of development spawned the greatest multiplier in terms of job growth and revenues that remain in the state and its localities.[34] Of course, many of the "big-box" retailers create jobs, but capture the revenues for owners in other locations. Many states, including Maine and many of its localities, will now begin to weigh the relative merits of job development and salary levels versus revenue retention and the municipal tax bases and the locality's ability to provide public services.

The state of Maine, in economic desperation, initiated a series of tax breaks to incentivize corporate locations to move to the state. The level of these programs then came under broad criticism within the state for being overly generous and plentiful while not resulting in sufficient returns to the people of Maine. Marc Breslow wrote a paper for the Commonwealth Institute in late 1999, the title of which tells the full story: "Economic Development Subsidies in Maine: Modest Job Gains at High Cost." In his study, Breslow notes the following:

- Maine taxpayers spent $40 million on corporate subsidies in 1998.
- Reports accounting for $33 million of that money were filed by 167 companies.
- Subsidized firms added 941 full-time jobs, but lagged behind state growth rates.
- The largest tax credits cost taxpayers $269,000 per job added in 1998, almost seven times the federal government's $35,000 limit.
- The major tax credits were more than one hundred times more expensive than the job training program, which cost only $2,300 per job added.[35]

States and localities will occasionally need to induce companies to locate or remain in a given area. However, these incentive schemes should be used sparingly and only when a clear return on the investment can be foreseen. Much more important in the long term will be the creation of a business environment that is friendly to companies and that will give them access to the workforce they require and the other assets and amenities they need to be successful.

3.6 Concluding Thoughts

There are two general types of economic malaise that can afflict a community: that which is beyond the control of anyone locally, and that which is self-inflicted. So-called smart growth policies could fall into the latter category or they can be supportive of growth generally while accomplishing other community objectives as well.

Smart growth is hard to categorize because it defies a fixed definition. I believe that smart growth—as I personally regard it in my community—is the best approach for capturing the benefits of economic growth without absorbing any more of the negatives than is absolutely necessary. The only problem is that, in my community and in most others, every hundred individuals can espouse fifty or more varying concepts of smart growth for the same community.

Each locality must decide for itself what parts of growth it wants, what it wishes to avoid, how to deal with the unwanted, unavoidable consequences of growth, and how best to control it. Again, local economic growth, and the decisions that can either enable, enhance, or constrain it, is all about balance. But whatever the decisions that are ultimately made for the community, it is vital that they be made and implemented when the general economy is strong. To wait until there is an emergency situation creates a situation in which success in building or sustaining the local economic base is doubtful. To sustain themselves through the bust periods, communities must be vigilant during the boom times. Slowing or stopping growth may have some merit at some times in some places, but localities must be careful what they wish for because it may just come true.

Notes

1. Shaffer, *Community Economics,* 1.
2. Bartik, "Economic Development Strategies," 95-33 (1995), 2.
3. Bates, *Alleviating the Lagging Performance,* 6.
4. Ibid., 1.
5. Downs, *New Visions,* 33.
6. Loveridge, "A Behavioral Approach to Understanding Local Leader Incentives in Economic Development," 8. The argument is offered by Loveridge that low-paying jobs are essentially "short-term" in nature and that higher-paying employment has more long-term impact. Although this is clearly correct, one must consider that many areas (1) are extremely grateful to get any jobs at all, regardless of the salary levels; and (2) that many areas do not possess the assets necessary to attract better-paying jobs. For those latter communities, the long-term focus must first be on the creation or attraction of those assets. In the interim period, lower-paying jobs may be the optimum targets.
7. Hevesi, "Smart Growth in New York State: A Discussion Paper," 3.
8. Ibid., 11. It may be a bit of a specious argument to maintain that the system of free enterprise allows people and businesses to determine the shape and nature of a community through the processes of supply and demand. One could easily counterargue that any individual and business reliance on their expressions of demand will ultimately shape the supply can be thwarted by the designs of land owners and developers who may primarily "supply" that which is most profitable.
9. Ibid., 3.
10. "What Is Smart Growth?" http://www.smartgrowth.org/whatis.asp.
11. Hevesi, "Smart Growth in New York State: A Discussion Paper," 25.
12. Flint, *This Land,* 86. The statement is made here that smart growth can only result when people are removed from their cars either to walk or to use mass transportation; however, most of the literature argues that multimodal transportation options create the greatest—and perhaps smartest—types of growth.
13. O'Toole, *The Vanishing Automobile,* 27.
14. Downs, *New Visions,* 4.
15. Hevesi, "Smart Growth in New York State: A Discussion Paper," 3.
16. Gillham, *The Limitless City,* 158.
17. Zovanyi, "The Growth Management Delusion," 2.
18. "Seattle Economic Trends," http://www.amlife.us/economic_trends.html.
19. Artz, "Rural Area Brain Drain: Is It a Reality?," 14.
20. Plosila, "Building Innovation-Driven Regional Economies in Small and Mid-Sized Metro Centers," *Economic Development America.* Washington D.C., U.S. Department of Commerce, EDA, 2005, 5.
21. O'Toole, *The Vanishing Automobile,* 187.
22. Ibid., 45.

23. "More Jobs?: No Thank You, Say Oregon's Mandarins," http://www.telegraph.co.uk/html.content.jhtml?html=/archive/1999/06/10/cuore10.html.

24. Ibid.

25. Gillham, *The Limitless City,* 218.

26. "Portland: Urban Growth Boundary Keeps Out Growth," http://www.demographia.com/db-pougbmivg.pdf.

27. Marshall, *How Cities Work,* 79.

28. Cortright and Mayer, "Spinoffs, Startups, and Fast Growth Firms in the Portland Regional Economy," 7.

29. Porter, "The Competitive Advantage of the Inner City," 11.

30. Cortright and Mayer, "Spinoffs, Startups, and Fast Growth Firms in the Portland Regional Economy," 12.

31. Timothy Priest, CEO of Greenlight Greater Portland, interviewed by Gerald L. Gordon (October 3, 2008).

32. "Outcome of Portland Experiment Still Uncertain," http://www.sprawlcity.org/portland.html.

33. Cohen and Garcia, "Learning from California: The Macroeconomic Consequences of Structural Changes," 13.

34. Http://www.newrules.org/retail/news_slug.php?slugid+360.

35. Breslow, "Economic Development Policies in Maine: Modest Job Gains at High Cost," i.

Chapter 4

Local Economic Recovery: Growth after the Fall

4.1 Can Losers Become Winners?

The question is really whether communities whose economies have experienced decline can make a comeback and whether, in the process, the lessons that were learned are transferable to other communities. Not only is the answer to the first query affirmative, but there are several examples from which to draw. The communities cited in this chapter, however, had a few advantages that helped in their return to economic well-being. First, each had a tradition of strong business practices, growth companies, labor forces with strong work ethics, and attitudes that generally supported their respective comebacks to economic stability.

In other words, this did not just happen as a matter of course. In each case, the local political leadership worked with their business communities and their residential communities as well as institutional partners in the community to correct the situations. The best minds looked forward rather than backward. In each case study, they built on what remained of the old economy while remaining focused on what was possible in the future. And, in each case, the reversals of fortunes required time and patience. The causes will be examined for the downturns, and the local reactions and results will be evaluated.

In this chapter, four such communities will be examined. To a very great extent, much of their economic decline resulted from an overdependence on either a single industry or a single employer: northern California and manufacturing, Pittsburgh and steel, Seattle and the Boeing Corporation, and Houston and oil. Each reveals important lessons for others trying to build or rebuild. The ultimate bottom line in each example is that those who have lost economic momentum can successfully rebuild. And, in each of these cases, the new economies are both diversified and have multiple clusters of employment.

And in each case, the local leadership set as targets the very industry clusters that have thrived and become the foundation for the new economies. In other words, none of this simply happened. These economies emerged as the result of active planning and reasoned strategies designed to create the very growth opportunities from which they are now benefitting. If it can be done in these exemplar communities, it can also be accomplished elsewhere.

4.2 Cluster Economies

A great deal of literature exists about the role played by business clusters in economic growth. This concept suggests that growth can be expedited and expanded by focusing on a community's comparative strengths. These strengths include the skill sets available in the existing labor pool as well as a wide range of other factors that are required either by business in general or by specific industries. Once an industry is identified that has a set of requirements for successful operations that are a match with what exists in a given community, that community has the ability to parlay those assets into business development not just for one business, but for many businesses and related organizations.

This is the concept of clustering. As an area gains more representation from an industry, it gains the ability to attract more of the same. It will also attract the associations and the suppliers and the infrastructure and the labor force that support the further growth of the industry. Groups will tend to cluster around what becomes a "critical mass" of people and operations, all related to a common cause or area of commerce. Over time, the primary industry is joined by suppliers, retailers, and buyers. Clusters gain strength by creating a self-contained product cycle in one place. The best employees can be attracted because there are many opportunities for lateral and upward movement on one's career path. Costs and time requirements can be reduced due to the proximity of suppliers and buyers.

A 2004 private study funded by the city of Seattle examined the impact on that city of the health care cluster. The report notes that clusters are generally composed of three layers: "a core of leading export companies and related industries; a layer of myriad businesses that provide supplies, specialized services, investment capital, and research; and a layer of essential economic foundation—advanced infrastructure, specialized work force training, research and development capability, and other directed public support programs."[1]

Clusters represent a means of increasing economic growth. Consider Morfesis' article (*Phoenix Business Journal*, January 31, 1997): "Arizona's economy is driven by twelve major industry clusters, ranging from agri-business to high-tech manufacturing. It is upon this plan that most cities and regions in our state have based their economic development plans and programs…Through this plan, we are acutely aware of our competitive strengths and weaknesses for companies in these twelve economic clusters." Communities, especially regions, that possess the necessary assets for a given industry, and that have a few companies in place, can target similar companies and additional support elements for continued business development.

Harvard's Michael Porter has done a great deal of the recent research on the effects of clustering. He maintains that it is both driven by and beneficial to competitive businesses. For one thing, cluster development results in new demand for support industries. This creates, in Porter's model, benefits that flow in both directions between businesses in the primary industry and those that support them.[2] A primary lesson for local economic developers that can be taken from Porter's work on cluster development is that one promising approach is the development of strategies that focus on what relevant industries require to evolve and succeed.

In another work—this one on competitiveness—Porter notes that there also exist clusters of clusters—overlapping clusters that "offer potential synergies in skill, technology, and partnership."[3] This presents new levels of opportunity for growth in local economies. Porter argues that localities can enhance the strength and effectiveness of clusters. This can be accomplished by ensuring that institutions and opportunities exist to promote interaction within and between the clusters by creating an environment conducive to small business start-ups, by targeting business recruitment outreach to specified clusters, by strengthening the local institutions that are important to the businesses of the cluster in question (e.g., K–12 education, higher education, physical infrastructure, research institutions, and more).[4]

To this list, I would add that it is important for local leaders to develop strategic plans and communications plans that establish the community as a home of these clusters in the eyes of the relevant business decision makers. The ultimate objective is to grow the business community and the wealth generated by jobs and employers. Decision makers must be made aware of the attractiveness of communities for their particular industry.

In this chapter, we will consider some regional economies where clusters that were both dominant and seemingly reliable, failed. Consider, for example, the business clusters in the Puget Sound region. Between March 2001 and March 2003, "fifty-six percent of regional job loss occurred in the target clusters. The largest—aerospace and information technology—experienced longer and more substantial periods of job loss."[5] We will observe the impacts of these losses and how, in each case, the region responded.

4.3 Case Studies

4.3.1 Northern California: Surviving Cutbacks in Manufacturing Jobs

California was a primary center of manufacturing in the United States for many years. By 1993, the level of unemployment in the state exceeded the national rate by one-third and was forecasted to climb again to one-half the U.S. average. Instead of adding a quarter million jobs annually as it had throughout the 1980s, California was now losing jobs—as many as 800,000—in under three years. From June 1990 to December 1992, California's job losses represented one-fourth of the national total. Cohen and Garcia noted that, "for the first time in memory, the California future looks worse than the California past."[6]

Adding to the state's woes were cutbacks in Defense Department procurement after the fall of the Soviet Union. While much of the pain was felt in Southern California, Dardia reported that where employment levels in the aerospace industry dropped by 40 percent between 1989 and 1994, the repercussions were felt statewide.[7]

In the Silicon Valley, the boom turned to bust. The Silicon Valley is generally defined as being "25 miles long and 10 miles wide."[8] Geographically, the Silicon Valley "encompasses the northern part of Santa Clara Valley and adjacent communities." It includes sixteen cities and an additional seven that are "sometimes associated with the region."[9] From the beginning of the decade of the 1970s, in the Silicon Valley, computer companies grew, including hardware and software manufacturers as well as integrators. As the industry grew, and more and more products and services became available, the venture capital community grew to take advantage of the opportunities and brain power. The first successful IPO, $1.3 billion by Apple Computers in 1980, drove additional growth in the local investment and financial industries.[10]

The region's cities had been greatly impacted by the growth of the economy following World War II. Increasing military expenditures in the region that continued to grow throughout the cold war, also helped to fuel the region's economy. "Sunnyvale, which was described as a 'quiet ranchers' trade center' with a population of 3,094, grew to a suburb with a population of over 107,000 by 1990…and, as late as 1970, San Jose was still classified as partly rural by the US census…by 1990, San Jose's population reached 782,248…and was the most populated city in the nation."[11]

But in November, 2001, Jon Swartz and Jim Hopkins wrote (*USA Today*, November 8, 2001) that the Valley "is in its worst slump in its fifty year history. It may not have bottomed yet. And, it is far from reclaiming its glory in the nation's economy." As the unemployment rose, the financial support for start-ups—in the form of venture capital—was down by 71 percent over the same point in the prior year. "September was the first month to pass without an initial public offering of any type."

What had happened to make the Silicon Valley the technology powerhouse that it was?

Most experts say that it was the culture of the companies in the Valley. Kanter wrote that companies in the Valley "operated a flexible, fluid network where job hopping, experimentation, collective learning, and risk taking were all encouraged." By the early 1990s, there were more than a quarter million technology workers in the region.[12]

And Cohen and Garcia emphasize that there was a healthy distribution of large and small companies. "Some of them, such as Hewlett-Packard, Intel, and Apple, have grown quite large, but the Silicon Valley culture and industrial structure is still that of a community of smaller, entrepreneurial firms."[13] It had always been the pace of innovation and the creation of new firms that fueled the economic growth in the region.

So, what caused the collapse? The Valley had been the home of nearly 7 percent of all U.S. patents issued in 1999, more than double its share at the start of the decade. But, in late 2001, 80 percent of venture capital investments were made to keep the companies in which earlier investments had been made from going under. And Swartz and Hopkins wrote (*USA Today*, November 8, 2001), companies were laying off tech workers by the tens of thousands: Cisco Systems, 8,000, and Hewlett-Packard, 7,000. The collapse was caused by a series of factors that came together coincidentally and included governmental, national, and international factors outside of the control of the Valley's business community or political leadership. The more salient question is really not how the collapse occurred, but how the recovery happened.

In the end, what brought the Silicon Valley back to technology leadership and commercial prominence in general were the qualities on which it was built it in the first place. Although that may not always help other communities that never had that kind of culture, it is instructive to consider what actually makes the Valley tick because the cultural implications may, at least in part, be replicated.

The first thing that must be considered to have given the Silicon Valley its impetus for growth was the ability of its companies to envision commercial applications for the technology they had developed and to pursue its privatization and sale. This is not always a typical outlook for scientists and engineers. All too often the solution of one challenge is seen by technological experts as a signal to seek out the next problem. The technology gurus of the Valley have grasped the commercial opportunities that are inherent in the products they have patented. While in many cases, this has meant the teaming of technology people with partners who were business-savvy, as frequently as not, it has meant that the technology person acquired the necessary business skills to mirror the technical skills. This requires not only a special, opportunistic technology person, but an environment in which such behavior is not only accepted but encouraged, celebrated, and rewarded.

A second asset of the Valley that enabled and supported the invention and commercialization of new technologies is the presence of a university that is effective in attracting research grants and federal support as well as delivering the training and retraining that support world-class technology exploration. Stanford is not unique in this definition, of course. Carnegie-Mellon in Pittsburgh, the University of Texas in Austin, and Baltimore's Johns Hopkins University in the field of biotechnology are just of few universities that have had similar energizing effects on local economic growth. Similarly, federal programs have served a like role in causing the commercialization of the technologies developed under contracts, including biotech companies around the National Institutes of Health (NIH) and the National Aeronautics and Space Administration (NASA)—both in suburban Maryland—and the Internet in Fairfax County, Virginia.

As its reputation for innovation grew, others wanted to join the elite businesses found in the Silicon Valley. "This led to a more competitive environment. The increased competition was an additional driver of the development of new technologies and higher quality products."[14]

A renowned university such as Stanford also plays a role in creating an aura about its general location. It creates a sense that, if one is to be a leader in technology business, one must at least consider a location in the Valley. MIT in Boston has a similar effect on site location decision makers. In this sense, the role of the university is one of helping to create the perception that the area is a world-class business location. "Stanford's successful recruitment of bright talent was followed by high technology firms seeking a source of innovative ideas."[15]

A lesson can be learned from this by other communities, large and small, urban and rural. Whatever the nature of the local industry, training and retraining will be important to the companies involved. Local colleges, community colleges, and trade schools can all help to build both the necessary reality that the community can provide what businesses in that industry require to grow, and the perception that, if this is the industry in which your company operates, this is one location you need to consider.

Another component of the success story that is the Silicon Valley is the presence of risk capital. However, one must be cautious of the chicken-and-egg argument here. The funding in northern California became available only after it became clear that good ideas were in the air and could be turned into high-return investments. Again, this can be accomplished in other locations where good ideas abound. It is for this reason that large venture capital communities have grown in Boston, northern Virginia, and elsewhere.

But, private risk capital is just part of the funding story. The Silicon Valley's investment community partnered with public officials to encourage the investment of pension funds, the creation of investment schemes through state and local governments, and the creation of a tax structure that encourages private investment in local companies. Local leadership can take similar actions to encourage public investment schemes and supportive tax ordinances.

Another part of the Silicon Valley culture that played a role in the growth of the business community is the presence of organizations that facilitate and encourage the interaction of the business leadership on a regular and meaningful basis. This encourages senior executives to discuss new directions and to coordinate their representation to the state and local governments. But there have also been forums for those same senior executives to interact with younger, up-and-coming business people. Even this very informal form of mentoring can have a significant impact on the creation and growth of young technology and other companies. And much of this came as the result of coordination with, and with the support of, local elected and administrative officials. Again, this can be understood and acted upon by public officials in any community.

One such organization has been Joint Venture: Silicon Valley Network. As Henton wrote, this network has "spawned a number of new networking mechanisms to help reconnect economy with community. The mechanisms include the Enterprise Network, which is helping new firms gain access to seasoned executive advisors," and others. "The pattern is the same in every case," he wrote. "Joint Venture: Silicon Valley Network is sustaining new social networks that bridge the economy and the community."[16]

Finally, the role of local government has been extensive in the Silicon Valley. "Businesses and local governments…are in a cooperative relationship. Several cities…have developed economic development strategies to help meet the needs of technology firms. Each developed innovative ways to become 'total quality' providers of government services and ensure that their regulatory processes are responsive. Mayors and local government officials in the Valley meet with technology firms on a regular basis and have reshaped local government service to meet industry needs."[17]

And industry has helped itself in forging relationships with the local elected leaders. "Silicon Valley Joint Venture…identifies and addresses issues that concern the corporate and residential citizens of the Silicon Valley…was formed in reaction to these challenges…Joint Venture worked with twenty-seven local governments in the region to streamline the local permit process, create a unified building code, and establish a 'smart permitting' system using the Internet. Finally, the organization created a social venture capital fund that helped local schools to improve student performance with the help of technology."[18]

The importance of the Silicon Valley's business culture in enabling and expediting its return to economic growth cannot be overstated. Schwartz and Hopkins (*USA Today*, November 8, 2001) quote Nathan Myhrvold, the former chief technology officer of Microsoft, as saying that the economy faltered, "but the engine of innovation is still humming." Is it possible for other communities to create their own corporate cultures?

4.3.2 Pittsburgh: Rebuilding without Steel

Pittsburgh represents a regional economy that has recovered from extraordinary losses in its predominant industry. It is also a story of a business culture that was central to its revival. And that revival ultimately resulted in the diversification of the traditional employment base as well as the retention of some elements of its previous economic long suit, steel. But, at its core, Pittsburgh's business culture was simply too tough to allow anyone to give up.

Lubove describes Pittsburgh as "a symbol as well as a city. It was synonymous with the spectacular advance of American industry, and the by-products: labor unrest, poverty, assimilation of a heterogeneous immigrant working force, and disruption of community cohesion. Pittsburgh was also the symbol for a broader metropolitan and regional complex whose one unifying force was business enterprise."[19]

By the conclusion of World War II, Pittsburgh had become the headquarters location for large corporations, including Westinghouse, U.S. Steel, Alcoa, and others. The future of the local economy seemed to be assured for generations to come. The Internet-based publication, *Citizendium,* provides an excellent summary of what happened to the steel industry cluster in Pittsburgh as well as the "reinvention" of the city and the region after the early 1970s. Pressure on the industry, once thought to be an eternal source of economic growth and power, came from a variety of sources, including foreign competition, the outdated technology of the local producers, labor costs and union issues, the 1973 oil crisis, and the substitution value of other materials.

Reagan-era deregulation piled on to the manufacturers woes and depleted local material supplies and the costs of transport of these resources spelled the death knell for the industry. "Beginning in the late 1970s and the early 1980s, the steel industry in Pittsburgh began to implode...The closures caused a ripple effect, as railroads, mines, and other factories across the region lost business and closed... Pittsburgh suffered as elsewhere in the Rust Belt with a declining population, and like many other U.S. cities, it also saw sustained middle class movement from cramped old housing to new spacious housing in the suburbs." (Lubove, *Twentieth Century Pittsburgh: The Post Steel Era,* 3.)

Lubove wrote that "the metals industry alone employed about 125,000 workers in 1960, representing two-fifths of manufacturing employment and one-seventh of total employment. The average manufacturing plant employed 109 persons, compared to the national average of 52."[20]

And Henton describes the situation in the region as its economic strength ebbed. "Erosion of Pittsburgh's iron and steel industry advantage caused...strong action by the early 1970s." A group (Penn's Southwest Association) was created "to attract new firms in other industry sectors to diversify the local economy further. After fifteen years in operation, the Association had attracted almost three hundred companies and thirty thousand jobs to the nine counties of the greater Pittsburgh region."[21]

Richard Florida notes that Pittsburgh had become to manufacturing R&D what the Silicon Valley was later to become to technology development. "Pittsburgh financiers and entrepreneurs largely spawned the American steel industry, the aluminum industry, and the modern electrical industry...Pittsburgh was also home to cultural and media innovations."[22]

By the end of that decade, however, as the region's one-time stranglehold on the steel industry fell prey to foreign competitors, the city's suffering worsened. "Recession and growing automotive imports lessened Detroit's demand for steel. Technological advances in steel-making lessened the industry's reliance on coal and iron...Global competition and environmental pressures also contributed to the decline of several large, integrated mills in the Pittsburgh region."[23]

By the early 1980s, the region's economy was in full-scale decline. In an article in a local paper a generation later, Christopher Briem (*Pittsburgh Post-Gazette*, February 16, 2003) recalls the conditions of the early 1980s. "The reality was that the region was facing an unprecedented abyss. National Guard units were being mobilized not to face an external threat, but to deal with domestic discord due to the dire economic conditions. Before it was over, the region would lose over 130,000 manufacturing jobs, taking with them the additional jobs that were indirectly supported by the mills and the earnings of their workers." Briem reported further that unemployment throughout the region had reached 18 percent and went as high as 28 percent in some communities. And people left town, taking with them the skills that would be needed to attract new industry. The precipitous declines in population can be seen closely in Figure 4.1.

Steel had not been the core industry in Pittsburgh; it had essentially been the only industry. Its dominance in the local economy, unchallenged for generations, left no opportunities and little hope in its wake. As Treado and Giarratani characterize the situation, "Pittsburgh's decline from steel preeminence was swift and painful...By the year 2000, employment in primary metals manufacturing had dropped to less than 2 percent of Pittsburgh's regional employment."[24] The extent of this impact can be seen in Figure 4.2, which demonstrates the sharp increases in total unemployment

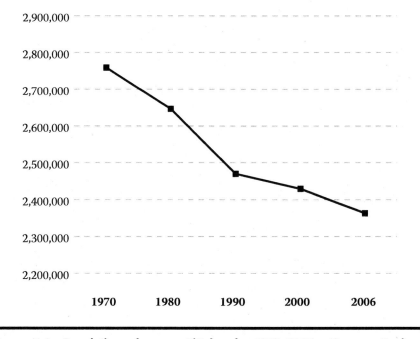

Figure 4.1 Population changes, Pittsburgh: 1970–2006. (*Source*: Regional Economic Accounts, U.S. Department of Commerce, Bureau of Economic Analysis, Washington, D.C., 2006.)

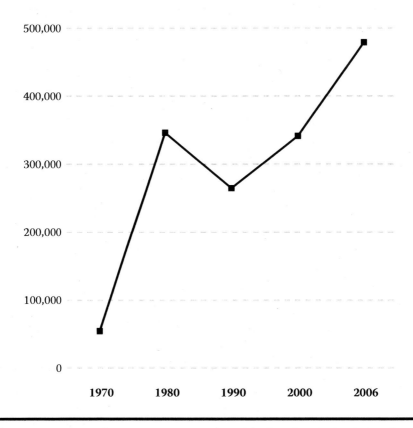

Figure 4.2 Unemployment compensation, Pittsburgh: 1970–2006. (*Source:* Regional Economic Accounts, U.S. Department of Commerce, Bureau of Economic Analysis, Washington, D.C., 2006.)

compensation in Pittsburgh through the latter part of the twentieth century. Between 1970 and 1990, the Pittsburgh region reflected the fifth greatest population decline among the nation's metropolitan areas. Among the country's metropolitan areas during that time period, the region had the ninth lowest increase in total income.[25] And Fitzpatrick (*Pittsburgh Post-Gazette*, July 15, 2001) wrote that "the Pittsburgh metropolitan area was the only one among the country's top thirty to lose population in the (1990s), declining 1.5 percent. Pittsburgh is also near the bottom of rankings among large metropolitan areas for the amount of annual immigration to the area and the percentage of foreign-born workers in its labor force." Without more immigrants, Fitzpatrick felt "Pittsburgh companies will have problems filling new jobs. Without new jobs, Pittsburgh will have problems attracting immigrants."

Yet, despite the depths to which the city and the region had plunged, the passage of twenty years revealed a different picture. Katherine Yung wrote (*Detroit Free Press*, April 14, 2008) that "Pittsburgh, like Detroit, had long relied heavily on one industry for economic growth and ignored warnings to diversify." But, in

April 2008, she reported that "thanks to expansions in health care and higher education, Pittsburgh now boasts more jobs than before the steel industry collapsed." *Citizendium* reports that, today, the largest private employers in the city are the University of Pittsburgh Medical Center (26,000 employees) and the University of Pittsburgh itself (10,700 employees) and is often cited as a highly "livable city." This prompted Plosila to call Pittsburgh "one of America's major rebirths."[26]

And although the essence of the recovery was based on the diversification of the economy into a variety of commercial areas, it did not require the community to turn away from its traditional strength completely. Many steel mills were converted either to new applications or retrofitted to include the new technologies that would enable them to be competitive in various specialty markets. And "Pittsburgh maintains important ties to the global steel industry through the continuing presence of a thriving community of intermediate suppliers to the steel industry."[27] These firms supply a range of products and services that includes raw materials, heavy machinery, and engineering and consultation.

Lubove references five economic sectors or clusters in which the Pittsburgh region "might emerge as a world leader. These five clusters employed 250,000 and produced 21 percent of salaries and wages: metalworking, chemicals and plastics, biomedical technologies, information and communications products and services, and environmental technologies."[28]

As was the case in the Silicon Valley, the community combined forces and both grew and attracted new and diverse industries, in part by capitalizing on three common strengths: institutions of higher education, public and private venture-backed financing schemes to promote entrepreneurialism and risk-taking, and the long-standing business culture of the region. As Lubove summarizes, "economic development was tied far less to the locational advantages that Pittsburgh had exploited in the nineteenth century. The region, therefore, could shape its own future, creating an environment attractive to the professional and scientific personnel upon which future growth depended."[29]

Pittsburgh has, for a community of its size, exemplary institutions of higher education. The most noteworthy of these include Carnegie–Mellon, which is renowned for its research in areas of information technology, and the University of Pittsburgh, well-respected for its medical center. As Richard Florida noted, "Pittsburgh attracts hundreds of millions of dollars per year in university research funding and is the sixth largest center for college and university students, on a per capita basis, in the country."[30] And these two universities alone have been the source of hundreds of technology companies in a variety of fields.

In a later chapter of this book, Florida's theories of the creative economy will be examined as they relate to the growth of local economies. It is useful to note at this point, however, that he maintains that Pittsburgh, with enormous opportunities physically surrounding the universities, failed to exploit their fullest potential to establish an early creative economic base. However, the universities were maximally utilized, as was the case in the Silicon Valley, both to support and drive business growth and to contribute to the overall enhancement of the city's and the region's images as good places to do business and research.

According to Lubove, the "Pittsburgh Renaissance was an extraordinary episode in American urban development. It had no precedent in terms of mobilization of civic resources at the elite level and wholesale environmental intervention."[31]

The shutdown of the steel industry in Pittsburgh had involved more than jobs. "Swept away was an intergenerational way of life that provided a sense of continuity, security, family cohesion, and communality."[32] But, as relates to the culture of this community, Yung (*Detroit Free Press*, April 14, 2008) may have expressed it best: "Don't underestimate the power of community spirit and pride. More than anything else, Pittsburghers' devotion to their city seems to have kept it from becoming a wasteland."

4.3.3 Seattle: Overdependence on a Single Business

Until the early 1970s, residents of Seattle would have been surprised had anyone forecasted serious economic difficulties for the region. After all, Boeing had been the mainstay of the economy, providing good pay, challenging work, and a secure future. No one could foresee either a decline in the company's fortunes or their own. However, that is precisely what happened. As the 1970s started, the favorite joke around town was aimed at the last people to leave Seattle: Please turn out the lights! As went Boeing, so went the entire region. As one writer (*East Bay Business Times,* October 1, 2004) put it, "Washington State's aerospace industry stands as a case study in how the decline of a dominant industry reaches into every facet of a region's economy."

Emmett Shear does a nice job of characterizing the extent to which the aircraft manufacturer dominated the economic landscape. "When the war ended, the military cancelled its bomber orders; Boeing factories shut down and 70,000 people lost their jobs."[33] The situation in the Pacific Northwest was different than in Pittsburgh in one way: the overdependence of the local economy was not due to a primary industry, but rather to a single employer. By 1957, nearly every other person in the region who was employed worked for Boeing. As Sharon Boswell and Lorraine McConaghy wrote (*Seattle Times*, November 3, 1996), "in 1970, the Puget Sound economy was still a one-trick pony." As the region grew, Seattle acquired suburbs, which grew at the expense of the downtown. Residents who could afford the suburban lifestyle chose it and the city declined.

In the less-than-two-year period from early 1970 to late 1971, the Boeing workforce was slashed from more than 80,000 workers to just over 37,000. As Shear wrote, "Seattle was hit perhaps harder than most due to its overreliance on Boeing as an employer—it had the worst post-Great Depression unemployment for any major city ever at nearly 12%. The cause? In the early 1970s, Boeing employed about 19% of the region's workers."[34] And, Boswell and McConaghy (*Seattle Times*, November 3, 1996) noted, "in 1970, the company began a 17-month period without a single new order from any U.S. airline. In March 1971, the U.S. Senate rejected further funding to develop Boeing's SST, the supersonic transport with commercial and military applications. Then, the energy crisis hit, driving up the cost of flying. Things that we historically took for granted as competitive advantages suddenly became less of a given."

As in Pittsburgh, the unemployment reached the high teens (17 percent) for the entire region. And, of course, layoffs at Boeing caused tremendous ripples in spending throughout the community. Boswell and McConaghy (*Seattle Times,* November 3, 1996) noted that "waves of layoffs rippled through machine shops and industrial suppliers, stores, and restaurants." But the reaction in Seattle was different from the reaction in Pittsburgh, according to Shear, where the population dropped dramatically and immediately. Pittsburghers simply left to find employment elsewhere. However, in Seattle, "despite the crushing unemployment, there was no massive outflux of people; it was never more than 15% of those laid off."[35]

The result was that, when national economic conditions permitted renewed growth, Seattle was well-positioned to recapture its share because it still had a well-trained and highly retrainable workforce present. Figure 4.3 and Figure 4.4 reflect

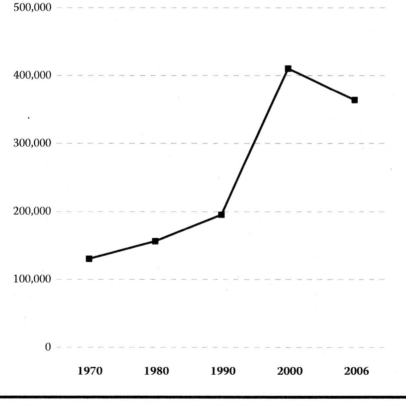

Figure 4.3   Unemployment compensation, Seattle: 1970–2006. (*Source:* Regional Economic Accounts, U.S. Department of Commerce, Bureau of Economic Analysis, Washington, D.C., 2006.)

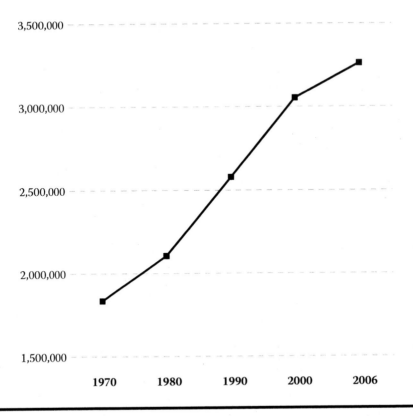

Figure 4.4 Population growth, Seattle: 1970–2006. (*Source:* Regional Economic Accounts, U.S. Department of Commerce, Bureau of Economic Analysis, Washington, D.C., 2006.)

the sharp increases in unemployment compensation at the same time the population continued to increase. And, indeed, between the years 1970 and 1990, Seattle enjoyed the fifth fastest growing total income among the nation's metropolitan areas. How did this happen?

It was the remaining highly educated and technically skilled labor pool that enabled the growth of Microsoft. It was the same labor force that supported the growth of smaller businesses in software and other areas of technology development. Its ease of reach from the Pacific rim gives the region a strong trading position and Seattle's economic base has become much more diversified than ever before, but Boeing remains the largest employer in terms of positions. In 2005, aerospace accounted for more than 40 percent of all manufacturing jobs in the Seattle Metropolitan Division. However, the industry represented only 4.4 percent of all nonagricultural employment, down from 18.8 percent in 1968. Distinct suburban office markets have emerged while the city remains "viable as a center of business, commerce, and industry."[36]

In 2001, Boeing announced the relocation of the corporation's headquarters to Chicago. For a time, it was unclear the extent to which this move would have any significant adverse impact on the region's overall economic image or draw as a business location. However, several years after the fact, it appears that no real damage has been done, as the region's growth in IT, biotech, and other clusters have demonstrated the economic advantages of a Puget Sound location. The highs and lows of the local economy, in relatively predictable cycles, have abated with the decline in the relative significance of Boeing jobs to the whole. "As the Seattle economy has expanded and diversified, fluctuations in employment and unemployment have tended to more closely follow the national economy."[37]

The diversification of the economic base of the Puget Sound region now also includes a strong health care cluster in the city of Seattle. This cluster encompasses health care delivery, biotechnology research, and training. It has, according to a funded study by the city, "propelled the economy forward by attracting substantial human and financial resources to the city...Seattle has the largest concentration of medical facilities and personnel in the Pacific Northwest." Today, one in five Seattle jobs is tied to this cluster, which contributes approximately $30 million to the local tax base. The same study estimates that, with spinoff (induced) employment included, the total number of cluster-dependent jobs in Seattle reaches more than 115,000.[38]

The other assets that supported the resurgence of the Seattle economy include some of the same things noted in the Silicon Valley: the presence of a strongly technology-based university, the willingness of private capital to invest in the commercialization of new technologies, strong public support for entrepreneurs, and a variety of mechanisms that encouraged the interaction of executives from companies large and small. As in Oregon, the state of Washington has attempted to direct development into a defined Urban Growth Area (UGA). "Of the new residential growth that occurred within the UGA since 1995, roughly half of it was absorbed by communities in the region's urban core in places that are typically well served by existing public facilities and services." The remainder has occurred in areas that are not as well served by the region's overtaxed infrastructure.[39]

Directly north of Seattle lie King County and Snohomish County. Snohomish County is a beautiful area whose leadership set out years ago not just to attract growth, but to attract the type of business growth they wanted and to site it in places that would complement the extraordinary natural views of their community rather than detract from them. In an interview, Deborah Knutson, the executive director of the Snohomish County Economic Development Council, stressed three main themes: the continued importance of Boeing to the region's economy, further diversification of the economic base, and regional cooperation for economic growth.

Boeing, according to Knutson, is not always fully appreciated by the residents of the region. The company has not only been a source of jobs for residents over time, but has also been a good corporate citizen, contributing to a wide variety of organizations in the community and directly impacting the overall quality of life. Conversely, losses of Boeing jobs over the years have meant a loss of support for community organizations that provide services ranging from the arts to health care to education. Although the percentage of the job base that Boeing represents is considerably smaller than in the past, the numbers are still quite large and changes can have very dramatic impacts, both positive and negative.

The Puget Sound region, once overly dependent upon this single employer and the single (aerospace) industry, has, in recent years, diversified its economic base and thus become more stable. In Snohomish County, more than 20 percent of the jobs are in manufacturing and they constitute over 40 percent of the region's total salaries, according to Knutson. So, there is still an issue of dependence; however, many of the county's working residents now travel south to Microsoft or elsewhere for work, and this means that fluctuations in the Boeing workforce do not yield such dramatic swings in the region's overall fortunes.

Even within the context of the manufacturing segment of the economy, Knutson cites a clear recognition that the stability of the future economy lies in developing the "next new ideas." For this reason, government and industry must work together to "stay on top of industry trends and determine what the businesses of the future will need, and industry needs to understand the issues and constraints of government."[40]

This implied partnership between the public and private sector is a cornerstone of the regional cooperation that Knutson has helped to foster. This cooperation extends from an interconnected economy and coordinated infrastructure development to regional promotion for business attraction and the growing emphasis on cultural opportunities. Knutson points out that, in part due to Microsoft and its spinoffs, the region is able to attract a highly creative workforce and, thus, highly creative businesses. All of this helps to grow and sustain the local economic base.[40]

A new regional growth strategy has been outlined in the Vision 2040 document that "expresses a preferred pattern and distribution for future growth that, when compared with recent trends, directs a greater proportion of future population growth to designated urban growth areas (93% total) and decreases the amount of growth allocated to the region's rural areas (7%)."

Puget Sound is a region that has either concluded that its growth is a positive or that it is unavoidable. Either way, the region has decided to take maximum advantage of the growth, to protect its natural resources, and to direct it rather than be led by it.

4.3.4 Houston: Diversifying the Economic Base

Like Seattle, Houston suffered through a confluence of events and factors that conspired to wreak economic hardship on the city, the region, and the people. The post-World War II years saw a revival of demand for housing and the consumer products that filled them. Industrial growth that had, during the war years, trebled, now continued with joblessness being diminished as industry was able to produce, obtain funding, and sell its products.[41] The pattern of urbanization taking place in the rest of the country emerged in the Houston region in the early 1950s as suburban neighborhoods grew that, with the exception of employment opportunities, were self-contained for shopping, living, and relaxation.

It was at this time that the need for attention to be paid to the growing needs of the urban core arose. "Already the problem of city and county financing were beginning to be felt."[42] The relationship of business growth to the general quality of life became more evident as the region began to emerge as an industrial power in the Southwest. But regardless of what other industries were able to take hold in the Houston area, oil remained king. "In 1946, the 6 percent of the land area of Texas that was in the 19 counties surrounding Houston accounted for 20 percent of the state's total crude oil production and 40 percent of its refinery capacity."[43]

Diversification of industry in Houston came to be seen not in terms of the oil and other industries, but rather as diversification within the various functions of the overall oil industry. Local economic stability had come to be seen as having the different phases of oil production and distribution all in the same locale because "the industry is a diversified one, with no prior record of depression striking all oil industry phases (including exploration and production, refining, transportation, and marketing) at the same time."[44] However, this confluence of functions was struck by a slowdown at the same time in the 1957–58 time frame, but growth in the local economy grew substantially in the other industry areas and sustained the region's overall growth until the phases of the oil industry were able to recover.

True diversification of the economy of the Houston region emerged in the decade of the 1960s as NASA established its Manned Spacecraft Center and Mission Control Center in the region. Throughout the decade, construction of these facilities alone contributed to the economic growth of the area and spun off considerable ancillary growth in the region. Between 1958 and 1963, Houston built twenty-three new major office buildings with more than 6.5 million square feet of space. "Houston built more office space from 1961 to 1965 than it had in its 116-year history through 1952."[45]

Throughout the 1970s, Houston enjoyed tremendous growth, both commercially and in the residential communities. Oil was king, and the king was healthy. However, by the early years of the next decade, the city suffered with the rest of the country through a serious recession as well as extraordinary fluctuations in the price of oil worldwide. Kotkin points out that, by the end of the 1980s, Houston's mid-town population had fallen to "less than a thousand largely destitute people; only nine of its 325 homes were owner-occupied."[46]

What had happened? A concise summary of the events that mark Houston's economic history is provided on the Web site Houstonhistory.com. A watershed in Houston's manufacturing growth occurred in 1973–74 when the production of resources lagged behind products available from around the world. Foreign production and federal regulation of prices deflated prices even though the supply was being diminished. However, the 1973 Yom Kippur War and OPEC production controls subdued foreign supply and began to drive up prices. This stimulated production in Houston and sustained the local economy for several years. However, Houston's economic stability took a hit in 1982 when oil-related employment began to decline. It reached 1,487,000 in August 1983, down from 1,642,000 in March 1982. The lesson learned was that "Houston's manufacturing base is considerably more vulnerable to downturns from international factors than most had suspected."[47] Like Pittsburgh and Seattle, the city managed its comeback by diversifying its industrial base. Oil would still be king, but a full and sustainable recovery would require a lot of diverse princes.

The result of Houston's comeback has, at least in part, been a story of a revitalized downtown. Whereas the economic recoveries of Pittsburgh and Seattle resulted in the growth of the suburbs more than the comeback of the inner city, Houston brought residents back into the core and re-energized life in the downtown areas. One must be cautious, however, in regarding changes in the number of residents because the urbanized area in which population is counted has also changed over time. Thus, observing the densities gives a more complete view of what happened. Table 4.1 provides the population data over time as well as the land area and the resulting changes in residential densities.

The Houston metropolis grew dramatically as the economy developed and the availability of good jobs in the petrochemical industry grew. And although the population continued to grow rapidly throughout the last half of the twentieth century, the region had the capacity to grow to accommodate it. And, in so doing, it maintained fairly constant densities in its neighborhoods.

At the same time that the region was expanding outward, the city also grew. By stretching the city's physical limits as the population grew, the densities within the cities changed little over more than fifty years, as is reflected in Table 4.2. As Kotkin noted, "inside the 610 loop, the freeway that surrounds central Houston, housing starts rose tenfold during the decade, with over 6,500 multifamily units constructed between 1996 and 1998."[48] This provides a sharp contrast to both Pittsburgh and Seattle where the decline of the downtown areas paralleled that of the economy. In 1983, Bernard and Rice noted the rise of an attitude supportive

Table 4.1 Population, Land Area, and Residential Density in Houston's Urbanized Area, 1950–1998

	1950	*1990*	*1998*
Population (×000)	701	2,901	3,434
Square miles of land area	270	1,177	1,537
Residential density	2,600	3,021	2,234

Source: Randall O'Toole, *The Vanishing Automobile and Other Urban Myths* (Bandon, Oregon: The Thoreau Institute, 2001), 501.

Table 4.2 Population, Land Area, and Residential Density within the City Limits of Houston, 1950–1998

	1950	*1990*	*1998*
Population (×000)	596	1,631	1,787
Square miles of land area	160	540	600
Residential density	3,726	3,021	3,000

Source: Randall O'Toole, *The Vanishing Automobile and Other Urban Myths* (Bandon, Oregon: The Thoreau Institute, 2001), 502.

of growth on the part of most Houstonians who "unite behind the policies of the community's business leaders." The culture and values of the city, they argued, "support the concept of unlimited economic opportunity…This consensus…enables the business community to pursue a policy of economic growth."[49]

Today, Houston's economy, although still largely dominated by the oil industry, has a variety of additional industries that are gaining strength, including aerospace, health services, biomedical R&D, engineering, manufacturing, and shipping through the Port of Houston, now one of America's most active international shipping gateways. The growth of these commercial areas has had an important stabilizing effect on Houston's economy and on its economic outlook.

A 2006 private study funded by the Houston Partnership listed the region's clusters as petroleum and petrochemical products, manufacturing, health care, professional services, aerospace, biotechnology, nanotechnology, and construction. The study also noted that "each job in the focused clusters is export-oriented, thus creating spinoff activity."[50]

However, the overall proportion of the economy that can be attributed to oil and petrochemical production and refining remains near 50 percent. As noted in a September 2000 report of the Federal Reserve Bank of Dallas, "apart from the boom and speculative excesses of the 1970s and early 1980s, this percentage has changed little in thirty years."[51]

In an interview with a Houston economic development official, Craig Richard, the Houston story became somewhat more clear.[52] The diminished dependence upon a single industry—oil and gas—is the result of years of conscious efforts to create an environment that would be conducive to business growth and that eliminates the dramatic swings in the local economic base. In the mid-1980s, the business leadership of Houston (at that time predominantly from the oil and gas industry) combined forces with the Chamber of Commerce, the Economic Development Council, and the World Trade Council to create the Greater Houston Partnership. Richard expresses with pride that the present board of that group includes many of the CEOs of the region's leading companies, including numerous Fortune 500s.

Says Richard, "They are on committees and are active; they are very committed to their community."

The program that has emerged in Houston focuses on creating an environment in which businesses can grow and be successful, and to which they want to locate. For this reason, incentives are not regarded as "a fallback" option. Create the right environment and they will come. He refers to it as an ecosystem for industries. Interestingly, part of the strategy includes playing off of the strengths of existing industries to create an attraction for others. For example, the oil and gas industry requires scientists and engineers with some of the same skill sets that have helped to build a large and thriving medical establishment in Houston. The Houston region has become, in Porter's terminology, a cluster of clusters.

In Houston, the business community has played a strong leadership role with the community's elected officials to assess their competitive strengths and determine how else to employ them. With such partnerships and such focus on the elements of the business environment, Houston has built a stable industry base that can now remain stable over time and fluctuations in the larger economy.

4.3.5 Concluding Thoughts

This chapter has considered local economies that suffered tremendous reversals from seemingly rock-solid bases of leading employers or industries to devastating job losses and general economic decline. These declines were so pervasive that the communities' entire ways of life were severely impacted. In situations this dire and unplanned for, the first question raised must be: Can they come back?

Can a community reinvent itself? Northern California, Houston, Seattle, and Pittsburgh have all done just that. Each now has a diversified, world-class economy that capitalizes on past strengths, and acquires and builds upon new assets and amenities. In some ways, this gives them the opportunity to build from the ground up and to incorporate into their plans several key components: economic diversification, cultural amenities, infrastructure, and educational and other strategic partnerships. In short, these newly economically vital communities have incorporated quality-of-life elements into their planning that complement the economic rebounds of their communities.

And in some cases, the businesses in the community that have common needs have developed into clusters. Much of this has occurred other than by design and we have seen how communities can help to spur economic growth within and around these clusters by helping to develop structures and processes for mutually beneficial interaction by both employers and employees. Atkinson and Andes take this strategy a step further by suggesting that companies can seek to "leverage external resources to complement internal research, development, and product commercialization efforts."[53] They note that "open innovation helps companies to partner to contribute expertise in their specific disciplines, to share cost and risk, to define problems more broadly."[53]

The concepts of clustering and open innovation are indicative of the fact that communities can advance their economic growth through the collaboration of the local private and public sectors. Local economic growth yields outcomes that are beneficial to all; and therefore all parties have a stake in the design and implementation of the process.

Still, the greatest lesson to be learned from these communities is that it can be done!

Notes

1. Huckell/Weinman Associates, Inc., "Economic Contribution of the Health Care Industry to the City of Seattle," 8.
2. Porter, *Competitive Strategy.*
3. Porter, "Clusters of Innovation: Regional Foundations of U.S. Competitiveness," xii.
4. Ibid., xviii.
5. "Puget Sound Trends," http://www.info@psrc.org.
6. Cohen and Garcia, "Learning from California: The Macroeconomic Consequences of Structural Changes," 3.
7. Dardia et al., "Defense Cutbacks: Effects on California Communities, Firms, and Workers," 5.
8. "A Brief History of Silicon Valley," http://people.seas.harvard.edu/~joues/shockley/silivalley.html.
9. "Stephen's Web," http://www.downes.ca/cgi-bin/page.cgi?topic=164 8.
10. Ibid., 4.
11. "Santa Clara County: California's Silicon Valley," http://www.ups.gov/history/nr/travel/santaclara/economic.htm.
12. Kanter, *World Class,* 205.
13. Cohen and Garcia, "Learning from California: The Macroeconomic Consequences of Structural Change," 4.
14. "High Technology Clusters in Silicon Valley," http://www.american.edu/academic.depts/h-sb/citge/silicon%20valley%202.htm, 2.
15. Ibid.
16. Henton, *Grass Roots Leaders,* 185.
17. "High Technology Clusters in Silicon Valley," http://www.american.edu/academic.depts/h-sb/citge/silicon%20valley%202.htm, 2.
18. Ibid., 3.
19. Lubove, *Twentieth Century Pittsburgh,* 2.
20. Ibid., 3.
21. Henton, *Grass Roots Leaders,* 186.
22. Florida, *Rise of Creative Class,* 305.
23. Treado and Giarratani, "Intermediate Steel Industry Suppliers in the Pittsburgh Region: A Cluster-Based Analysis of Regional Economic Resilience," 10.
24. Ibid., 3.
25. Downs, "Major Shifts in Population and Economic Activity," 16, 20.

26. Plosila, "Building Innovation-Driven Regional Economies in Small and Mid-Sized Metro Centers," 4.
27. Treado and Giarratani, "Intermediate Steel Industry Suppliers in the Pittsburgh Region: A Cluster-Based Analysis of Regional Economic Resilience," 2.
28. Lubove, *Twentieth Century Pittsburgh*, 257.
29. Ibid., 135.
30. Florida, *Rise of Creative Class*, 216.
31. Lubove, *Twentieth Century Pittsburgh*, 137.
32. Ibid., 8.
33. Shear, "Booms and Busts," 6.
34. Ibid., 6.
35. Ibid., 7.
36. "Seattle Economic Trends," http://www.amlife.us/economic_trends.html.
37. Ibid.
38. Huckell/Weinman, "Economic Contribution of the Health Care Industry to the City of Seattle," 2.
39. "Puget Sound Trends," http://www.info@psrc.org, 1.
40. Deborah Knutson, executive director, Snohomish County, Washington, Economic Development Council, interviewed by Gerald L. Gordon, October 2, 2008.
41. "Years of Readjustment (1945–1950)," Houstonhistory.com, 1.
42. Ibid., 2.
43. Ibid., 2.
44. "Years of Consolidation," http://houstonhistory.com, 1.
45. "Years of Diversification," http://houstonhistory.com, 2.
46. Kotkin, *The New Geography*, 53.
47. "Our Legacy," Houstonhistory.com, 2.
48. Kotkin, *The New Geography*, 53.
49. Bernard and Rice, *Sunbelt Cities*, 205.
50. Perryman Group, "Paths to Prosperity: Strategic Job Growth Parameters for Opportunity Houston through 2005," 7.
51. "Houston Business—A Perspective on the Houston Economy," http://www.dallas-fed.org/research/houston/2000/hb0006.html
52. Craig Richard, senior vice president, Opportunity Houston, October 20, 2008.
53. Atkinson and Andes, "The 2008 State New Economy Index," 58.

Chapter 5

The New Growth Economies: Attracting and Retaining the Local Business Base

5.1 Making the Pro-Growth Case to Local Elected Officials

The heading of this section is intentionally misleading. It is intentional because this is the way that many growth advocates think about their challenge. How can we convince decision makers and the community that commercial growth is a positive? It is misleading because growth, of itself, is simply a means to an end. The real questions, then, must be: How can we illustrate to decision makers and the community that the benefits of commercial growth are so considerable that the rising economy will indeed lift all boats? How can we demonstrate that the resulting revenues will not only minimize the cost burdens of public services for residents, but will generally enhance the quality and quantity, as well as the breadth, of those services, thereby enhancing everyone's quality of life?

Now that we have the right questions, and are clearly focused on the ends rather than the means, what are the answers? Well, of course it isn't going to be *that* easy. The answer is different for every community, and is likely going to be different for the same community at different times. And without doubt, there will be times and places where the answer is negative.

But the question remains how to demonstrate to elected officials the positive advantages of commercial growth and the expansion of the overall economy. The consideration of this question must begin with the circumstances and needs of the particular community at that particular point in time. Starting from the premise that local elected officials, although concerned about their ability to retain their seats in the next election, are first sincerely motivated by what is best for their communities, one must first consider the communities' needs.

Local economies may, to an extent, be seen as living organisms. They are born, they grow, they get sick, and they can get better. Sometimes they try and sometimes they give up; and sometimes they try but fail. Often they need to absorb the costs of a growing population. We have seen how the demise of small, family operated farms drove families to metropolitan areas to seek employment. This generally means such an expansion of demand for schools and public services that the tax burden on residents must increase. We have also noted that, as urban areas grew and matured, they developed suburbs; and the suburbs became the areas to which the businesses were attracted, leaving inner cities with more pressing public service needs, but fewer and fewer of the higher salaried residents who could afford to pay the resultant tax bills. Cities and suburbs grew to support different types of arguments for commercial growth.

For the inner cores of urban areas, the arguments have become abundantly clear. As a result, they are the targets of less anti-growth or slow-growth movements than are the suburban and exurban areas of this country. For the central cities, one clear argument is that the revival of the downtown business communities will create jobs for the existing residents and that this will have a dampening effect on both unemployment compensation and other transfer payments as well as the types of behaviors that result in the rise of public service costs such as public safety. Moreover, growth of the downtown employment base will have the effect of bringing residents back into the city core in search of the types of lifestyles they cannot find in the suburbs. Indeed, as urban economies benefit, so benefits the physical landscape. Communities are revitalized and neighborhoods improved, and the overall quality of life can be enhanced, the importance of which to business attraction and retention efforts cannot be overstated. As these trends occur, a stronger labor force may be brought back and, as Cortright and Mayer wrote, it "helps start-up firms to have a richer supply of technically trained labor than they might otherwise enjoy."[1]

The arguments supporting commercial growth in suburban and exurban areas are more diverse and often less effective. This should not be too surprising: over the past several decades, the outer rings of metropolitan areas have been the sites of residential growth and commercial expansion. Businesses could find cheaper land and facilities and a more proximate, more well-trained and highly motivated workforce. Indeed, over time, as the inner suburbs became more like the downtown core, the subsequent rings of growth—the exurban areas—became the true suburbs. And with that came the growth of the next stage of commercial development and the resultant wealth.

But with that growth also came questions about its impacts on the existing quality of life because what also came was sprawl; and sprawl has led many an American community to resist further commercial development. However, what has become clear to many regions in the United States is that new residents will continue to migrate to metropolitan areas. In so doing, they will create demands for schools and roads and parks and libraries and human services and the whole array of public services that are inflating local budgets across the country. Given that they will continue to arrive, local elected officials frequently will be receptive to, if not in agreement with, the argument that the rising costs of public services cannot be addressed solely by placing the tax burden on residents. Further, it is a generally accepted principle that businesses take back far less in public services than their tax dollars pay for. Residents, on the other hand, reverse that formula, generally using up far more in public service dollars than they pay in the form of various taxes and fees. This makes the argument for commercial growth much more palatable to elected officials.

Regardless of the purposes of economic development programs, the optimum way to make the case to elected officials relates to performance measurement. Elected officials are responsible to their constituents for the decisions they make regarding the allocation of scarce resources among competing public service demands. Practitioners need to demonstrate why expenditures to promote the enhancement of the local economy are wise. This can best be accomplished by establishing the program objectives in the strategic planning process, determining how best to measure the relevant outcomes, setting up the systems necessary to capture the data, and determining how best to communicate the resulting data to the relevant audiences. By clarifying the objectives and reporting the results on a regular basis, constituents gain an ongoing appreciation for the program and its objectives, its operations, and its activities; and local elected officials gain cover for the difficult decisions they must make.

5.2 Marketing at Home and Abroad

Communities that are active today in economic development attempt to grow their local economies in a variety of ways, including business attraction, business retention and expansion, and business start-ups. It has become increasingly important to do so with an eye toward international commerce. Locally produced goods and services are today, more than ever before, either comprised of, or produced with, foreign equipment or other inputs, or have the potential to be marketed outside of the United States. Companies that become active in U.S. markets can be found in every state and region and even in many cities and towns.

This makes the marketing of goods and services outside of U.S. borders a realistic local growth strategy for most communities. It also means that approaching foreign-owned businesses to expand into U.S. communities may have merit as a local growth strategy. Of course, this can be accomplished in several ways. Most states, and some larger cities and counties, especially border communities, have mechanisms in place for international marketing outreach. Fairfax County, Virginia, maintains five permanent offices in overseas locations (London, Frankfurt, Seoul, Tel Aviv, and Bangalore) to market the county to technology businesses interested in expanding into U.S. markets. Smaller communities, which may not have the same level of resources, can approach marketing through other agents, including local banks, law firms, or other organizations with global reach. Many of these community institutions have offices, employers, or clients in locations throughout the United States and around the globe, and are often willing to use their good offices to assist the locality by making introductions, providing insights and intelligence on the markets, providing meeting space or distributing materials, co-sponsoring events and even representing the community, either formally or informally, to potential prospects.

And, of course, most U.S. states have overseas representatives, in specific markets, who tout either the advantages of conducting trade with, or doing business in, their states. In a world where the value of international commerce will only increase, there will certainly be an increase in competition for the sale of similar goods and services. This will result in a naturally driven trend toward businesses and communities succeeding in international marketing on the basis of their greatest comparative advantages. This means that, for localities to expand their economic base through global outreach strategies, they will need to identify that which they do better than others and focus on the increased effectiveness of those industry sectors.

The lessons for communities, then, are to enhance the efficiencies of the industry sectors in which they have comparative advantages and develop the infrastructure they need to succeed. As noted previously, this may include workforce development, education and training programs, supportive local regulatory and tax policies, and national and global outreach to companies in the identified clusters.

5.3 A Tale of Two Cities: A Comparison of Long Island, New York, and Fairfax County, Virginia

In early 2007, the *New York Times* published an opinion piece about a publication called "A Tale of Two Suburbs" (*New York Times*, April 1, 2007). In that piece, Douzinas et al. wrote that "when local taxes grow so burdensome that they drive away the young professionals that businesses need, a region loses competitiveness." Given the seriousness of the situation confronting Long Island, the comparisons were made with another large suburban jurisdiction, Fairfax County, Virginia, a suburb of Washington, D.C. In a sense, the communities had much different histories. Fairfax County was, in the 1950s, the leading dairy producer in the Commonwealth of Virginia. Its population grew between 1950 and 1970 from fewer than 100,000 to more than 454,000, a 360-percent increase.[2]

The more mature Long Island already had significant and growing populations Between 1950 and 1970, the combined populations of Nassau and Suffolk counties grew from just under 950,000 to more than 2.5 million, nearly 160 percent.[3] However, further comparisons illustrate similarities and the differences. Douzinas et al. (*New York Times*, April 1, 2007) list the following as some of the distinctions:

- Both are large suburban areas proximate to major cities.
- Long Island (Nassau and Suffolk counties) was about three times as large in population (2,762,551 compared to 996,176 in Fairfax County).
- Long Island is larger in area (1,199 square miles compared to 395 in Fairfax County).
- The density of population on Long Island and in Fairfax County was similar: 2,304 and 2,522, respectively.
- Both had high household incomes: $75,177 on Long Island and $88,133 in Fairfax County.
- Median home values (2004) were relatively equal: $394,682 on Long Island and $415,418 in Fairfax County.

But this is where the comparisons got really interesting. The following comparisons between these two seemingly similar jurisdictions make it clear that they are, at least in the sense of the local economic growth, two completely different places. Consider these additional facts:[4]

	Long Island	Fairfax County
Total number of municipalities	439	17
Total school districts	127	1
Number of taxing authorities	900+	5
Property taxes per capita (2002)	$2,450	$1,547

What had happened to the economy on Long Island was easy to understand. In the 1970s, Grumman removed thousands jobs and the economy of Long Island was left irreparably damaged. The communities did not pursue business development to replace the jobs and the area became essentially a bedroom community for New York City. Without the business tax dollars to help the 439 municipalities pay for the public services demands that were increasing, the burden was placed instead on residents. Today, the tax burdens are so great that an extraordinary proportion of the residents wish to leave, but cannot afford to do so because they may not be able to sell their homes. In 2006, that survey indicated that a whopping 54 percent of responding residents wanted to leave Long Island! Douzinas et al. (*New York Times*, April 1, 2007) further note that those who can leave do so, including many of the young people whose skills and talents will be necessary to attract new businesses should the effort ever be rejoined.

In terms of economic growth, the distinction between the two regions has been that Fairfax County has had it and Long Island has not. The Long Island Index reports that, for the ten-year period from 1996 to 2006, growth of the regional Gross Metropolitan Product (GMP) for northern Virginia was double that on Long Island: 89 percent growth for northern Virginia, compared to 44 percent for Long Island. Further, "with an economy spawning jobs, northern Virginia residents have a higher average per employee salary (based on 2006 figures): $52,815 compared to $43,264 on Long Island and $41,299 for the United States overall."[5]

By contrast, Fairfax County has been able to play off its strengths to grow a thriving business community that is engaged in a wide range of technologies. The traditional strengths of Department of Defense and other federal contractors have been complemented by leading companies in information technology, telecommunications, aerospace and aviation, biotechnology, and more. There, a rising tide has indeed lifted all boats. Foreign-, minority-, and women-owned businesses thrive and contribute. And although the population has grown from 455,000 in the late 1970s to more than one million today, the real estate tax rate, which comprises nearly two-thirds of the county's general fund in a $3.4 billion annual budget, declined from $1.74 in 1976 to $0.92 in fiscal year 2009. When asked if they thought they could trust their respective county governments to do the right thing most of the time, 51 percent of northern Virginians responded affirmatively while only 26 percent of Long Islanders did so. And 79 percent of northern Virginians had a "very" or "somewhat" favorable opinion of their county government while only 64 percent of those on Long Island did.[6]

Fairfax County is clearly a new-growth economy. Through the 1950s, it was the largest dairy-producing jurisdiction in the Commonwealth of Virginia. Today, Fairfax County has, among the nation's large communities (those of 100,000 or more residents), the highest median family income, the lowest crime rate, the lowest unemployment rate, and arguably the best schools in the United States. What made it work was a strategic vision that was based on the understanding that the forecasted population growth could not be stopped and that focused on the growth of the local business community to help provide jobs and pay for the public services that the growing residential community would demand. Finally, the vision and strategy were only as good as the commitment to adhere to it and to fund the economic development effort consistently. Over time, the return on that investment has proven to be tremendous.

Due to the extraordinary number of school districts, each with redundant buildings, staffs, and superintendents, the expenditure per pupil on Long Island

($17,392) is considerably greater than that in northern Virginia ($12,023), with its single school district serving nearly 170,000 children (2005–06). Yet, in a clear demonstration that spending does not always equate directly with quality, one list (*U.S. News and World Report*, 2006) analyzed 18,790 public high schools across the United States and included three from Fairfax County in the top one hundred, including the Thomas Jefferson High School for Science and Technology in the number one spot. Another list (*Newsweek*, 2006) included fourteen of Fairfax County's high schools in the nation's top 3 percent, including five in the top one hundred. That list included all fourteen of the public high schools in Fairfax County and only thirty-six others from throughout the rest of the United States.

In a summary statement, the reports' writers noted that the residents of Fairfax County are "twice as likely (62%) as Long Islanders (33%) to feel that the value they receive from property taxes in terms of the quality of local services was 'excellent' or 'good'." Douzinas et al. (*New York Times*, April 1, 2007) wrote, "three out of four Fairfax residents think things are going in the right direction in their county...Long Island comes in at 48%." If nothing else, the process and the commitment are lessons that can be, and have been, transferred to other communities throughout the United States.

5.4 Other Case Studies

5.4.1 Austin: University-Generated Growth

Austin, Texas, provides an excellent example of the role a college or university can play in a community's economic revival. As Henton noted, the University of Texas has "shaped key competencies around the directions of the regional economy."[7] But, such was not always the case. Prior to the mid-1980s, "the city was hostile to growth. The university, the state's flagship with fifty thousand students, was not a player in economic development. The nucleus of technology companies was small."[8]

But growth would come to Austin regardless of the city's desire for it. In 1969, the city's population had stood at just over 300,000. Every decennial census thereafter registered remarkable growth. From 1960 to 1970, the population increased by 32 percent, then by another 47 percent by 1980, 45 percent by 1990, and 48 percent by 2000.[9] By 2007, the population of Austin had increased by 28 percent and reached a total of 1.6 million. Looking forward, the Austin Chamber of Commerce reports that further growth is expected to bring the Austin population total to 1,655,883 by 2010 and to 2,154,682 by 2020. This represents increases of 32 percent between 2000 and 2010 and another 30 percent in the ensuing decade.[10] This dramatic population growth of Austin and its suburbs is illustrated in Figure 5.1

In a mid-2008 interview with Brian Hamilton, an Austin economic development official, it was noted that the issues of growth did concern city officials and residents, many of whom thought the city was growing too fast. Early "smart

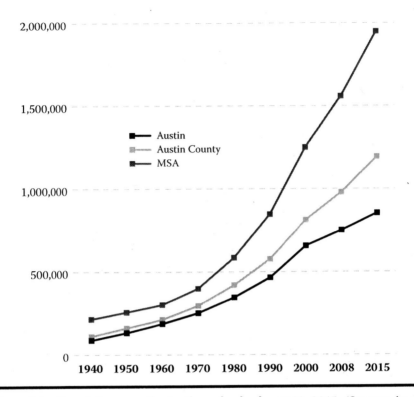

Figure 5.1 Population growth, Austin and suburbs: 1940–2015. (*Source:* Austin Area Population Histories and Forecasts. Department of Planning, City of Austin, April 2008.)

growth" policies adopted by the city council evolved into economic development policy. For instance, to protect an aquifer zone west of the city, economic development incentives were offered for and promoted only on the east side of town. Moreover, the city council once went as far as to correspond with Fortune 500 companies to discourage locating facilities in the area.[11]

Nonetheless, the region's population continued to grow. As the suburbs emerged and evolved, the preponderance of the growth moved into the northwest and northeast suburbs, creating such heavy demands for services that affirmative efforts were made to bring residents back into the city. Large downtown housing projects helped to revitalize the core, thus relieving some of the pressure on the areas to the north. At the same time, city officials and the private sector worked to bring retail and nightlife options into the city. The resultant agglomeration of restaurants, jazz clubs, and retail establishments has created a highly renowned quality of life that has made the city increasingly attractive to both residents and businesses that are interested in accessing the young people who enjoy the lifestyle and the presence of the university. This regeneration of the Austin downtown led Richard Florida to call it "a leading center of the creative economy" that "consistently ranks among the top regions on my indicators."[12]

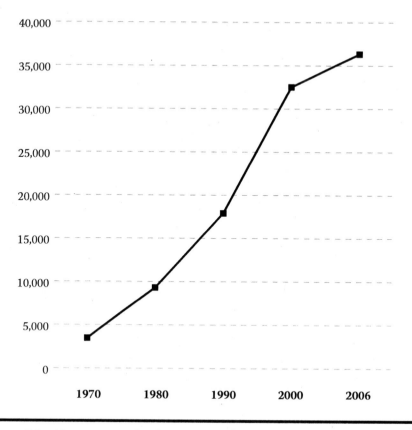

Figure 5.2   Mean per capita income, Austin: 1970–2006. (*Source:* Regional Economic Accounts, Bureau of Economic Analysis, U.S. Department of Commerce, 2007.)

However, unlike some other cities in which an influx of residents generated dramatic increases in the unemployment rate, Austin, between 1980 and 2000, saw an increase in the number of jobs and a decline in their levels of joblessness.[13] And the rate of people in poverty declined from 15 percent in 1989 to 10 percent in 2000.[14] With a growing job base came substantial increases in wealth. Figure 5.2 illustrates this in terms of growth in the mean per capita income levels between 1970 and 2000, before beginning to level off. Indeed, between 1960 and 1990, metropolitan Austin enjoyed the thirteenth fastest growing population, but the seventh fastest growing total income base among the nation's major metropolitan areas.[15]

What changed the posture of the region was, in the words of Smilor et al., the emergence of a technopolis: a region "that interactively links technology development with the public and private sectors to spur economic development and promote technology diversification."[16] They continued to write that the creation of a technopolis requires three essential factors: the achievement of scientific preeminence through the receipt of R&D grants or the attraction of Nobel laureates, the development and maintenance of new technologies for emerging industries, and the attraction of major technology companies and the creation of homegrown technology companies.[17]

Of course, local economic growth on this scale does not simply occur. In Austin, the chamber of commerce set out to attract businesses to the region. A five-year, $14 million fund was collected, only $350,000 of which came from the several municipalities in the region. A second five-year phase generated $21 million in investments. The objectives were both jobs—attracted and retained—as well as wealth generation. Only about one-third of the costs of public services in the city come from real estate taxes (both residential and commercial). Another fourth comes from sales taxes and an additional 19 percent from water and electric utility transfer fees. Economic growth of various types thus contributes to the ability of the city to provide a high quality of life while minimizing the burden of the costs on residents.[18]

Of course, being a university town enabled the city to attract a young workforce. Today, Austin enjoys a very young demographic. Much of what was accomplished came as a result of conscious efforts to coordinate with the University of Texas in Austin and to allow it to identify and play its role in supporting and leading the city's growth in various commercial technology sectors. Smilor et al. have listed eight ways in which the university was a critical component of Austin's growth; these are roles that institutions in other communities have and can play as well by

- fostering research and development activities;
- contributing to perceptions of the region as a technopolis;
- attracting key scholars and talented graduate students;
- fostering the spinoffs of new companies;
- attracting major technology-based firms;
- nurturing a large talent pool of students and faculty from a variety of disciplines;
- acting as a magnet for federal and private sector funding; and
- providing a source of ideas, employees, and consultants for high technology as well as infrastructure companies, large and small, in the area.[19]

Still, economic fluctuations were in store for Austin, which had diversified the base of technologies and the sources from which technology companies emerged, but had not sufficiently diversified the region's economy in other (nontechnology) sectors. An analysis by Market Street Services in 2003 reported that, by 2000, "technology sectors accounted for over two-thirds of Austin's traded sector income...with an extraordinary reliance on the information technology industry, Austin has a highly undiversified economy which makes it vulnerable to downturns...No industry is likely to be able to replace jobs lost in information technology and manufacturing."[20]

Following national trends in the technology sectors, Austin began to lose jobs—a total of 25,000 (or 3.7 percent) between November 2000 and March 2003. And the region's per capita income fell during that same period by 4.5 percent.[21] To reverse this situation requires time and a gradual diversification of the general economic base to match that which has occurred in the technology sectors. Only such diversification away from one, or a few, industry sectors (including public employment), or a prominent large employer, such as Dell, can provide economic stability through recessionary periods or downturns in specific industry sectors. This is an important lesson for any community, regardless of its current economic well-being.

The lessons Austin offers for other cities that are either pursuing or experiencing substantial economic growth include the development of a quality of life that is attractive to both employers and the workforce they need, the full utilization of local institutions of higher education, and the expression of an attitude of being open for business.

Austin has effectively used its enhanced quality of life in the downtown to attract and retain young, creative workers and the businesses that need them. A 2001 article from the National Governors Association states that "government leadership in Austin recognized early that its unique cultural environment was a competitive asset to the new economy. Through deliberate and strategic action, Austin has built a world class high technology economy on the base of a thriving cultural center recognized for its outstanding quality of place."[22]

5.4.2 Las Vegas: Policy-Making to Encourage Growth

Following World War II, the Las Vegas region saw numerous resorts begin construction. Contrary to popular belief, the development of the now-famous "Strip" took place not in the city limits of Las Vegas, but also in neighboring Clark County. In fact, by 2007, nearly 72 percent of all Nevada residents lived in Clark County, compared to less than 56 percent in 1970.[23] This has created some interesting regional dynamics, but the real dynamics that control growth are the exercise of various state and federal government controls over what happens in the region.

The addition of gambling casinos, popular entertainers, and other amenities made the city boom. Larger and more spectacular resorts and casinos were planned and developed. By the mid-1990s, Las Vegas could boast of having thirteen of the world's largest resort hotels and more than 88,000 hotel rooms.[24]

In a 2008 interview with two economic development officials of the city, it was noted that the original development of these projects was considered to be quite risky. As other parts of the United States also began to develop gaming industries, there was a concern in Las Vegas that the region would become little more than one among many. However, the density of gaming operations, complemented by the growing entertainment industry in the region, began to create the brand that the city enjoys today as the mecca for gaming enthusiasts.[25]

Table 5.1   Population Growth, Hotel Rooms, and Gaming Revenue in Las Vegas, 1980–2008

	1980	*1990*	*2000*	*2008*
Clark County population (×000)	463	684	1,429	2,049
Number of hotel rooms (×000)	45.8	73.7	124.3	137.0
Las Vegas visitor volume (millions)	12.0	21.0	35.9	40.3
Clark County annual revenues (millions) from gaming	$1,617	$4,104	$7,571	$11,039

Source: University of Nevada at Las Vegas, 2007.

Over time, one can observe the direct correlation between the growth of the hotel industry and the increases in population, the volume of visitors to the city, and the gross revenues derived from gaming. Table 5.1 provides the comparative data and Figure 5.3 through Figure 5.5 illustrate dramatic growth in population, per capita income, and total employment from 1970 to 2006. In fact, Anthony Downs noted that, between 1960 and 1990, the population of Las Vegas and the surrounding metropolitan areas grew faster than any other metropolitan area in the country and enjoyed the third fastest growth in total income during that same period.[26]

Such intense growth does not occur without creating problems. According to its critics, Las Vegas has allowed the gaming industry to control "other civic activities from the center to the margins." Tourism now occupies the geographical core of the region; so, too, does poverty. Other traditional downtown features like shopping areas, cultural centers, sports venues, and business headquarters are "chaotically strewn across Las Vegas Valley...Meanwhile, its suburbs stubbornly reject integration with the rest of the city."[27]

By the turn of the millennium, the city had begun to pursue two parallel initiatives: the need to attract office space users to the region and the redevelopment of areas of the core. The structure of regional controls has played a large role in how the city has evolved and how it will evolve in the future. The state of Nevada maintains strong control over the use of revenues and the lands surrounding the city and much of its suburbs are controlled by the federal government. Much of the contiguous lands have been sold for development and there is very little left for the city to control when making economic development plans. This has had effects on growth similar to urban growth boundaries and has meant that regional officials have had to turn their attention inward. The result has been infill projects and redevelopment programs to maximize use of the land that is available and over which they can still exercise development control.

In a manner reflective of the great American spirit, the region has taken a position of learning and benefitting from the significant environmental challenges it

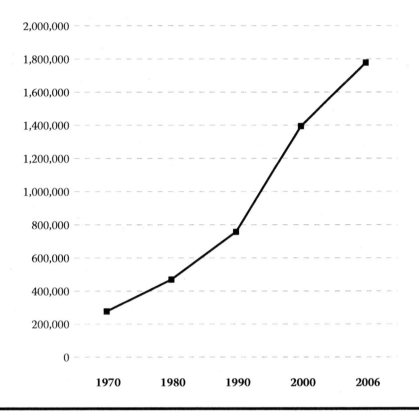

Figure 5.3 Population growth, Las Vegas: 1970–2006. (*Source:* Regional Economic Accounts, Bureau of Economic Analysis, U.S. Department of Commerce, 2007.)

has had to confront. Now a region of more than two million residents, Las Vegas has been forced to learn how to provide water and services; construct infrastructure; and erect churches, retail outlets, parks, and more as rapidly as the population expanded. The lessons learned from this experience as well as the lessons learned from existing in the desert have led the region's entrepreneurs to begin to consider how best to create a truly sustainable economy in other locations. Officials now expect to develop and export industry strengths in those sectors.

5.4.3 Phoenix: Rising in the Southwest

As preparations for World War II increased, Phoenix became the site of several military facilities and some of the defense support industries that were useful to the local bases. As noted in an earlier section, further impetus for growth came to Phoenix as the Sun Belt grew as a result of manufacturers leaving the Northwest and the Rust Belt and heading for the warmer climes of the South and Southwest. In doing so, they created new cities and regions.

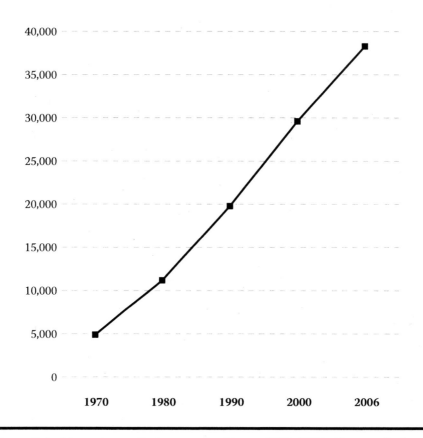

Figure 5.4 Mean per capita income, Las Vegas: 1970–2006. (*Source:* Regional Economic Accounts, Bureau of Economic Analysis, U.S. Department of Commerce, 2007.)

Before the war, Phoenix's employment base was under 45,000. A paper by Elliott Pollack describes how the military leadership of the day believed that coastal manufacturers could be targeted and began to move them inland, thus further benefitting the Phoenix area in terms of employment and economic growth.[28] Following the war years, the plants that had been producing military hardware turned to defense and civilian production. But the economy was also able to diversify, even within the general realm of manufacturing. "Other types of manufacturing eventually took to the area, especially electronic firms that flourished in the low humidity climate that was so necessary to their success." Between 1948 and 1960, 300 more manufacturers came to Phoenix to take advantage of the climate and the workforce, thereby creating an additional 15,000 new jobs in just twelve years.[29] Figure 5.6 and Figure 5.7 illustrate the substantial and constant growth in Phoenix' total employment and mean per capita income levels from 1970 to 2006. Further, during the cold war, "military installations such as Luke Air Force Base

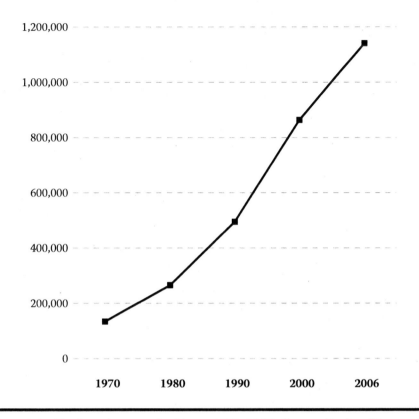

Figure 5.5 **Total employment, Las Vegas: 1970–2006. (*Source:* Regional Economic Accounts, Bureau of Economic Analysis, U.S. Department of Commerce, 2007.)**

and Williams Air Force Base continued to serve as part of the national defense effort, and former war plants looked not only to the military, but to civilian markets as well. A multiplier effect took hold, and as more manufacturers moved to the area, they attracted others."[30]

City officials acted to encourage business growth. As a right-to-work state, the lack of union involvement was attractive to businesses, and the state legislature moved, in 1955, to repeal sales taxes on products manufactured for sale to the federal government. "The day after the legislature acted, Sperry Rand headquarters in New York announced that it would definitely locate its electronics aviation division plant and research center in Phoenix."[31] The city had not only made itself attractive to business development through a specific action, but it had generally promoted its general openness to, and support of, economic growth.

As the employment base grew, so grew the region. The region, between 1960 and 1990, enjoyed the seventh fastest population growth among the nation's largest metropolitan areas.[32] But its growth has been "far different than that of the traditional manufacturing regions of the Rust Belt. The residential density of central

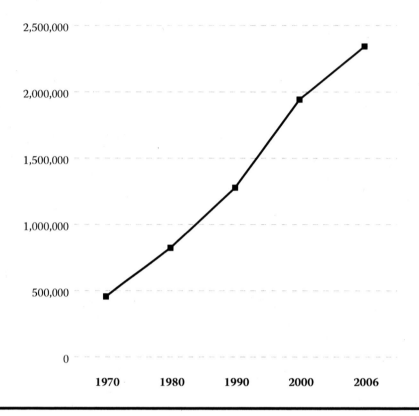

Figure 5.6 Total employment, Phoenix: 1970–2006. (*Source:* Regional Economic Accounts, Bureau of Economic Analysis, U.S. Department of Commerce, 2007.)

Phoenix is extremely low compared to any older city, but its suburbs are scarcely less dense than its center."[33] However, further growth in the Phoenix region is, and has always been, entirely dependent upon the ability of local officials to deliver water to its residents. To protect the relatively scarce land within the ring of development to which water can be delivered, city officials have been aggressive about purchasing open space and preserving it.

Phoenix is really a story about peoples' willingness to seek solutions to grow. "Despite its limited water supply, constrained land availability, and underdeveloped transportation system, Arizona has successfully managed to become one of the fastest growing states in the country."[34] As a result, the economy diversified further, adding a number of luxury resorts in the last thirty years of the twentieth century. In the end, the local economy has been stable over the years and has accommodated the growth that the region has enjoyed. As Pollack concluded, "we are not without problems. But, growth provides the tax revenues to deal with the problems." Phoenix is a prime example of growth welcomed, planned, and accommodated.

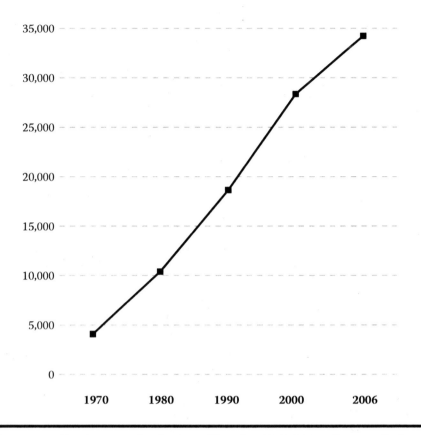

Figure 5.7   Mean per capita income, Phoenix: 1970–2006. (*Source:* Regional Economic Accounts, Bureau of Economic Analysis, U.S. Department of Commerce, 2007.)

5.5 Rural Economic Growth: Are There Unique Lessons?

To this point, the discussion has been largely within the context of urban areas and the suburban and exurban extremities. It is also important to consider whether any of the lessons learned in those contexts are also applicable to the rural communities around the country or whether those realities portend different conclusions for economic growth. As the president of the Northwest Area Foundation noted, "America is in the middle of a transformation of its rural areas. It does not have time to find perfect or guaranteed solutions. It must take the best ideas where it can find them and begin to adapt and adopt these ideas."[35]

What makes rural communities essentially different in the pursuit of economic growth are access and size. Businesses require certain sets of assets and amenities in the communities in which they locate. They require a certain amount of workers with certain sets of skills. They need to be able to reach their markets with relative ease. They may require more or less land or land at more reasonable costs. Some of these factors enable rural communities to attract the interest of businesses while others represent barriers. A mid-1990s report by the Federal Reserve noted that many rural communities were adding jobs at a faster rate than the nation's metropolitan areas, but that the jobs being added were at much lower rates of pay.[36]

"Innovation in a rural context may be as much to do with overcoming the obstacles created by geography and distance in accessing markets and resources as with the products themselves."[37] In many cases, however, the rural areas that added jobs were able to do so by providing support functions to major metropolitan areas from which they were sufficiently distant to provide lower cost, but also close enough to minimize travel or transport time and expense. These communities, as has been noted, also provide less expensive labor for functions that do not require density of population. In this sense, America's rural communities were the forerunners of the outsourcing issues of a later day vis-à-vis places like India and parts of the Far East.

Small towns in rural settings have a variety of issues to address when planning for economic growth. In 1999, I facilitated a strategic planning retreat for a rural county in North Carolina. This is an area that had suffered through downturns in markets for their agricultural crops as well as successive natural disasters. To prepare for the planning process, a survey was conducted in which citizens were asked to identify perceived impediments to economic growth.

The issues that were identified as hindrances to local economic growth ranged from concerns about leadership and teamwork to the costs of electrical power and zoning practices. Also mentioned were cultural needs, community appearance, and the need for more cultural outlets.[38] Not surprisingly, this lovely community was more critical than any visitor would have been. The point made, however, was that the survey responses provided the town and its leadership with a road map of what needed to be done to attract and retain businesses in the community. From there, it was a matter of prioritization and implementation.

Small communities that have some initial industrial presence have an advantage to use in growing their local economies. By taking the approach to clustering that was addressed in an earlier section, rural communities can create hubs of businesses and support services around a specific industry or industry segment. As Henry and Drabenscott suggest, "the rural areas that grew in the 1980s tended to be those with a head start in a vital industry."[39]

Another economic growth strategy for rural areas is to enable the development of entrepreneurs in the community. In an article prepared for the Federal Reserve Bank in Kansas City, Jason Henderson lists a number of key strategies for rural areas to consider when trying to create an environment in which entrepreneurs can grow and thrive. These include accessing venture or equity capital to invest in local entrepreneurs, educational programs to encourage and support entrepreneurship, and organizational networks to recognize and celebrate their efforts and their successes. He also suggests that communities can develop incubator facilities, often with the assistance of federal or state grants that will assist budding business people by sharing costs and creating an environment in which their shared experiences can benefit everyone.[40]

Various manufacturing sectors can represent special opportunities for rural areas. "Firms that thrive in the absence of agglomeration economies are those that do not require frequent face-to-face contacts with suppliers, markets, and competitors and that do not require a highly skilled or specialized labor force."[41] These types of operations, which are typically later in a product's life cycle, are often the targets of rural economic development professionals; however, rural areas must be sure that they continue to upgrade the locally available technology infrastructure to retain these employers.

Rural areas and small towns often may also have business assets in institutions of higher education, including community colleges and trade schools, that can help drive economic growth. Such was the case in Lenoir County, North Carolina, which relied heavily on the local community college to help the community's economy recover from natural disasters and the loss of jobs to build a new economy. The issue of availability of well-trained talent as well as a convenient location for skills upgrading and retraining is critical to communities trying to entice employers to locate to, or remain in, their areas.

A very thorough analysis of smart growth in rural communities was produced in 2002 by the Northeast-Midwest Institute under a grant from the U.S. Environmental Protection Agency. Its author, Barbara Wells, asserted that, because some believe that the supply of land in such areas is seemingly inexhaustible, and because such communities often lack formal comprehensive planning processes, growth can often occur without community endorsement. As a result, rural communities have begun to "mobilize around their concerns about growth and its effects on traditional town centers, natural resources, and working landscapes."[42]

One of the key issues relating to rural economic growth is the status of main streets in small towns. As the establishments along these main drives through town decline, the entire feel of the community changes. Visitors are left with an impression of decline and even despair that will be described to others. This will, of course, lead to a further decline in visitation. A variety of grants and programs exist to assist small towns in these situations, but they require someone to identify the opportunities, acquire the grants and programmatic support, implement the programs, and promote the changes. These are resources that are not always available directly *in* small town communities. They are, however, generally available *to* small town officials from state government representatives. The first step for small communities is to identify the resources available that will help acquire the other resources that can help make a difference. The second step is to marshal community support in carrying out the objectives of the project. Over time, dramatic differences can be effected that will benefit merchants and the town in general, and can help revive a sense of pride in the community.

Wells also maintains that rural communities can be susceptible, in the absence of strong comprehensive planning mechanisms, to sprawling commercial, resort, or residential developments that are unsightly. Often, at the beginning of the review of such projects, an initial enthusiasm may occur over the mere fact of something happening. However, over time, it may become apparent that the project, as designed, "leads to unnecessary environmental impacts, taxes the capacity of country roads, and saps the economic vitality from existing main street stores."[43] She further states that the maintenance of working landscapes need not be left to the landowners to protect that which we all wish to enjoy, even if only periodically. The federal government and state governments have acknowledged a responsibility to the protection of these natural landscapes and have numerous programs designed to assist communities. But again, communities must gather their human resources and make the case for grants and assistance; and must be prepared to put in the time and effort to protect their towns and the surrounding areas.

Relatively higher levels of unemployment in the nation's small towns are only part of the problem. Not included in the counts of the unemployed are those who either work part-time or who work at levels significantly below those for which they are trained and make much less in salary than they are qualified to make. These are the so-called "underemployed" who are counted in such surveys simply as employed. These are the individuals who have skills to market and are the most likely to move on to larger employment centers to seek better career opportunities.

This is a form of the brain drain that has already been described in some of the metropolitan areas reviewed in earlier chapters. These men and women also comprise the best asset a rural area has to attract employers. But, as Federal Reserve Governor Mark Olson said, "communities in rural areas can affect their economic future by understanding the changes that have occurred in rural America and adjusting to them."[44]

Another strategy that has had mixed results in different states has been to form partnerships between a state's stronger economic regions and its regions in need of economic growth. In such cases, many support and back-office operations can be performed in-state by a reliable and available workforce. One program that has had numerous successes for more than twenty years is the Virginia Economic Bridge Program, which connects the technology businesses community in northern Virginia with the rural communities of southwestern Virginia. Over the course of many years of discussions and relationship-building, the two communities have learned where the opportunities lie and have concluded a number of successful deals that have accrued to the benefit of all concerned. The community gains jobs and the businesses get productive, close-by support.

Although some may be inclined to leave the rural setting, others are clearly attracted by the lower costs, the absence of congestion, the slower pace, and the frequently natural beauty of such settings. Today's technologies allow many individuals to work from home, a trend that also makes a rural lifestyle possible. Communities can seek to attract these men and women, many of whom are entrepreneurial in spirit, by touting more broadly the benefits of their particular quality of life and their lower costs of living. Rural communities can take advantage of this strategy through promotions in urban and suburban areas to the creative class. As McGranahan and Wojan noted, "despite an urban affinity, the creative class…can be drawn out of the cities to high-amenity rural locations…Rural areas lack the business and consumer services available to urban businesses and residents, but rural areas tend to have the upper hand in landscape, which may service the creative temperament."[45] In short, communities need to market their comparative strengths.

And a 2001 article by the National Governors Association notes that the arts should not be ignored as potential contributors to local economic growth in rural areas. "Thriving tourism and cultural destinations are growing…latent artistic and cultural resources and contributing to economic sustainability in rural communities and regions. Cultural activities attract tourists and spur the creation of ancillary facilities, such as restaurants and hotels, and the services needed to support them."[46]

5.6 Regional Economic Growth: Are There Unique Lessons?

When seen in the context of regions, economic growth is more than simply the sum of the municipal parts. Certainly, total jobs can be counted, as can be total job gain or loss. Gross regional product can be calculated and conclusions regarding the direction of regional growth can be reached. But the factors that distinguish one region from another, and that are the source of the most discussion and debate, and that may have the greatest impact on the region over time, relate to internal dynamics between neighboring communities.

Regional growth must, therefore, be evaluated from three separate perspectives: that of the individual jurisdictions that comprise the region, their total economic performance, and the interplay of issues between the component communities. Most of the issues that affect the interest of businesses' location decisions and even their ability to succeed will come from one of these three perspectives.

The immediate host community is important to businesses because they set tax rates and approve local ordinances that can be more or less supportive of companies. They provide the location, in which they work, and its housing, schools, safety, and more. The host community is the home of an array of businesses that share the benefits of co-location and often create a positive environment for commerce: a "buzz."

Businesses also realize that regions are the sum of the individual parts. It is the region, not the host locality, that provides the workforce and a full variety of housing and lifestyles that attract a wider range of potential employees. Training and retraining opportunities are regionwide, not just immediately local. We have already seen that most of the commercial construction of the past generation has been in the suburbs rather than in the center cities. We have also cited Richard Florida's work on the creative economy, which argues that creative workers are attracted to the opportunities that often exist in cities rather than suburbs. Regions offer a wide range of lifestyles that permit people to enjoy their lives and their work.

The economic development practitioners in the Puget Sound region of Washington state have collaborated on a clear competitive advantage in acting regionally. "First, we must begin to think and act like a region. That is the driving force behind our participation in the Regional Partnership, a broad-based, bipartisan coalition that is formulating an economic development agenda for the three-county metropolitan region. The local economic development professionals, Kendall, Knutson, and Schunemann (*Puget Sound Business Journal*, May 9, 2003), are Regional Partnership supporters and have put aside partisan, ideological and geographic differences and are working together to improve our economy."

Anthony Downs itemizes the social and economic functions of the central cities within regions as causing creative contacts among top leaders, hosting specialized activities and facilities (e.g., cultural, sporting, and retail locations), and acting as the hub for area networks.[47] It is in the area of the interplay between jurisdictions over matters of common interest that businesses see the importance of the region as being greater than the sum of its parts. Transportation networks, clean water, the availability and location of affordable housing, open space, waste management, even crime are issues that do not stop at municipal borders. The ability to address these matters effectively on a regionwide basis is of great importance to the business community. To accept this, one needs only to count the number of regionwide organizations in any given metropolitan area. Councils of government, boards of trade, consortia of universities, and committees of all types of focus meet regularly. Once those lists have been secured, read the list of attendees that is inevitably addended to each report. It will include a range of participants that generally includes broad representation from the business community, and often at very high levels. Businesses clearly appreciate the regional implications of the issues being reviewed.

Often, regional leaders—public and private—will gather to support the revitalization of the downtown areas. This is in recognition of the fact that such areas, while in disrepair, radiate poverty, poor school performance, and crime, some of which will ultimately extend outward. City problems often become suburban problems; thus, the region will feel the need to assist in their resolution. There is also the matter of a region's image. Businesses do not want to remain in regions known for poor educational attainment, decaying cores, or as "murder capitals." Those who can leave often will, creating a corporate counterpart to the brain drain.

Henton et al. summarized the importance of regionalism to the business community. "The confluence of four forces in the last two decades of the twentieth century is increasing the importance of economic community…Fundamental economic, technological, demographic, and political shifts push collaboration at the regional level to the center of a new paradigm."[48] But perhaps the greatest intraregionally active force is the mobility of the labor force. In 2006, Fairfax County, Virginia, had 527,464 working residents and 506,272 jobs. Still, less than 53 percent of working residents remained in the county for work each day. More than 45 percent of the jobs in the county were filled by workers migrating in each day.

There is a fine line, however, between cooperation among a region's component jurisdictions and the sacrifice of one's competitive advantage for economic growth for the good of the whole. As Hevesi noted, "most local governments rationally want to maximize their tax base and minimize their service needs, and these specific goals often supersede regional concerns."[49]

As has already been noted, individual jurisdictions require economic growth to help provide for public services to their constituents without overburdening their residents with the resultant costs. This calls for cities and counties to pursue economic growth at home while enhancing the ability of the region to attract, retain, and grow businesses. But this does not mean sacrificing one's own economic growth to enable a neighbor to improve their own status. Economic development is a highly competitive endeavor and needs to be seen clearly for what it is.

The essence of regionalism as it applies to economic growth has its strength in one of two contexts. The first is that a region's component jurisdictions can sacrifice their individual business attraction efforts to a collective program. Phoenix, for example, recognized a glut of competing economic development programs that were having the effect of creating a poor showing to business prospects. "Internecine competition was also apparent during the region's failed attempts to lure two companies that were considering locating in greater Phoenix, with Semantech, an electronics consortium, locating in Texas, and U.S. West locating an R&D facility in Colorado." [50]

The second approach to regional economic development that is helpful is when the jurisdictions combine efforts for specific elements of the effort. Washington, D.C., at one time had earned a reputation that was not conducive to business attraction, or even business retention. Over time, as the city began to resolve many of its problems, the Greater Washington Initiative was created to announce to the world that the city and the metropolitan area were good places to do business. The promotional piece of that campaign benefits the entire region. There is not necessarily the need to develop business prospects for the participating jurisdictions in such partnerships. It is both an accomplishment and a great contribution simply to enhance the region's image in support of the outreach efforts of the twenty-one individual jurisdictions, all of whom either benefit or suffer on the basis of the reputation of the region's core.

Quite often, regional groups overlap with the functions of their component jurisdictions' economic development programs. This does not necessarily mean that there are redundancies, but the regional organization needs to ensure that it provides a service that the individual jurisdictions do not or cannot provide for themselves. Such functions can be identified even in areas where there are many jurisdictions that are active in economic development. As an example, the Greater Washington (D.C.) Initiative serves to promote business location to a region in which there are three states and more than twenty localities that have economic development functions. However, what none of those jurisdictions does individually is to promote the Washington area as a whole as a good place to do business. In a region that is still erroneously considered by many to be little more than a "government town," such general promotional efforts are a necessary and important complement to the efforts of the individual localities in marketing themselves to specific business prospects.

Regionalism does not always work and cannot always be forced. The Washington, D.C., area has all the components to be a leader in the areas of bioscience and biotechnology. Although it does indeed have a significant presence, it does not always compete well with the Silicon Valley or Boston for businesses in those sectors. The assets are all there—an existing base of bio companies, well-known assets including the National Institutes of Health in Montgomery County, and the Howard Hughes Medical Institute at Janelia Farms in northern Virginia. It has a world-class community of scientists on the Maryland side of the Potomac River and the IT base that is world-class in bio-informatics on the Virginia side. But the two neighbors are not connected in their marketing outreach to the industry so other regions with the same or even lesser assets in total appear superior because those assets are marketed and represented to the business community collectively. This is one area where regional programs can be increasingly effective and even more efficient.

There are those who call for regional governments, but that is not the argument being made here. The thesis here is simply that some issues call for regionwide collaboration and cooperation, and that businesses have a stake in the outcomes. Another argument that has been offered is that the economic comeback of regional cores should be either seeded by, or funded in its entirety by, publicly driven efforts and resources. Although some seed funds for general projects may have a positive impact on urban areas in need of commercial renewal, Porter is entirely correct in his assertion that "a sustainable economic base can be created in the inner city, but only as it has been created elsewhere: through private, for-profit initiatives and investment based on economic self-interest and genuine competitive advantage."[51]

Just because businesses share in the desire for improvements in the core does not mean that they will locate there. The basis of their decisions will be profitability. Regionalism and corporate participation in projects toward that end will ultimately be based on their presumption that an improved regional core is to their benefit. At a minimum, it must not come at a cost. Core cities, therefore, attract economic development and sustain their economic growth by creating a setting that is attractive to businesses and in which they can maximize their profits or reach a qualified workforce. "We must stop trying to cure the inner city's problems by perpetually increasing social investment and hoping for economic activity to follow."[52]

For inner cities to achieve economic revitalization and growth will mean that the basic foundations required by businesses must be created. Issues related to public safety, business and personal services, scores in the public schools, business associations and support groups, and general appearance must be resolved. Businesses will gather where it makes financial sense for them to do so, not where the communities most need the help.

5.7 Starting up Start-Ups

Inner cities have one resource that can be used to advantage when pursuing economic growth: the skills and talents of their residents. Programs that support the creation of businesses by unemployed and underemployed residents of core cities have the potential to result not only in the creation of jobs and income, but also can have an impact on crime, school performance, and other social problems. Communities often establish incubator facilities to assist these start-ups. These programs provide shared services to start-up businesses to reduce costs and contribute to a sense of community and shared experience between entrepreneurs facing common questions and business challenges.

When businesses are solid enough to "graduate" from the incubator programs, they are often ready to occupy commercial office space and thus contribute further to the neighborhood's revitalization. Often, businesses from throughout the region will contribute to these kinds of programs because the sacrifices required by men and women to get new businesses started and made productive is something to which they are more attuned than addressing social and infrastructural issues.

Can locally developed incubator programs be successful in spawning new jobs and companies that can stand the test of time? Earnshaw (*Portland Business Journal*, July 21, 2006) quoted what the National Business Incubation Association reported in 2006: "North American incubator companies have created about 500,000 just over the past 25 years (2006); that 87% of companies that have graduated from incubators are still in business—an extraordinarily high survival rate for small businesses."

There are other steps that local officials can take to support the growth of start-ups. Cortright and Mayer argue that "new firms are created by redeploying the intellectual and human capital that already exists in a region. The founders, managers, and workers that form new companies are drawn overwhelmingly from the ranks of the region's current workforce."[53] As will be seen in some of the later case studies, localities can facilitate the growth of start-up companies simply by taking steps to provide opportunities for this kind of interplay between local executives, and between local executives and local entrepreneurs. A strong local government–business community partnership in all areas of city or regional life can also contribute mightily to the perceived local culture as "a good place to do business." This is clearly an area where aggressive local policies can indirectly influence the pace, consistency, and stability of growth.

Finally, start-up businesses are often daunted by the difficulty and costs associated with the formal initiation of a business. Michael Porter maintains that these issues serve to stifle inner city entrepreneurship and place unnecessary barriers in the way of start-ups. "Restrictive licensing and permitting, high licensing fees, and archaic safety and health regulations create barriers to entry into the very types of businesses that are logical and appropriate for creating jobs and wealth in the inner city."[54] Inner city officials, then, can encourage the start-up of new businesses by reviewing their permitting, licensing, and other processes as well as the time frames required to negotiate those systems, to ensure that they are supportive of all entrepreneurs and are conducive to local economic growth.

5.8 Concluding Thoughts

Often, when local economies grow quickly, the community reaction is mixed. Some regard the changes to be ruinous of their lifestyle and community while others see the changes as being important for their futures. Still others will be uncertain or will regard some change as positive, but will want to draw a line in the sand because the impacts—both positive and negative—of local economic growth are so pervasive in communities that there are fewer issues that cause greater debate. This, in turn, means that local elected officials are especially attuned to development activities. And that means that they are constantly lobbied from many quarters regarding the necessary decisions to be made.

Elected officials make their living by weighing decisions one against another. What is in the best interests of the community? Which decisions will bear benefits that will exceed their costs? What policies will yield greater benefits than others? And even this: which directions will attract more support from constituents/voters than others?

Communities that have experienced rapid growth, like Fairfax County, Austin, Las Vegas, and Phoenix, have each confronted these questions. And each has sought the best balance between costs and benefits, between relative benefits of various policy decisions, and between voter support and opposition. In each case, vital economies and quality communities have been created. Long Island, too, had done so and lost some of its relative advantages and strengths. Today, their communities are actively engaged in efforts to recapture those advantages.

From a tactical perspective, regions, rural communities, core cities, and suburbs all have different assets to market. From the perspective of vision, however, there is less distinction. Economic growth can generate the good things in life: jobs, expendable income, better public schools and other public services, and a generally improved quality of life as well as economic stability and security. The challenge is to capture its benefits and minimize the negative elements. As has already been seen, strong leadership and adherence to a solid plan can make it happen.

Notes

1. Cortright and Mayer, "Spinoffs, Startups, and Fast Growth Firms in the Portland Regional Economy," 10.
2. Fairfax County Economic Development Authority.
3. Long Island Power Authority, 4.
4. The Long Island Association, "A Tale of Two Suburbs," 1.

5. Ibid., 3.

6. Ibid., 8.

7. Henton et al., *Grass Roots Leaders*, 27.

8. Ibid., 43.

9. "Historical Census of Housing Tables," http://www.census.gov/uues/www/housing/census/historic/owner.html.

10. "Austin," http://dporter@austinchamber.com.

11. Scott Hamilton, director, Las Vegas Economic Development, and Romeo Betea, interviewed by Gerald L. Gordon, August 7, 2008.

12. Florida, *The Rise of the Creative Class*, 217.

13. Market Street Services, "Economic Performance, Austin" (May 27, 2003), 3.

14. Ibid., 8.

15. Downs, *New Visions*, 18.

16. "The Austin/San Antonio Corridor: The Dynamics of a Developing Technopolis," http://www.utexas.edu/depts/ic2/pubs/corr, 22.

17. Ibid., 3.

18. Scott Hamilton, director, Las Vegas Economic Development, and Romeo Betea, interviewed by Gerald L. Gordon, August 7, 2008.

19. "The Austin/San Antonio Corridor: The Dynamics of a Developing Technopolis," http://www.utexas.edu/depts/ic2/pubs/corr, 6.

20. Market Street Services, "Economic Performance: Austin," 10.

21. Ibid., 8.

22. National Governors Association, "The Role of Arts in Economic Development," 7.

23. "Historical Economic Data for Metropolitan Las Vegas," http://cber.unlv.edu/snoutlk.html

24. Las Vegas Online. "History of Las Vegas," http://www.lvol.com/index/hist/lvhist.html.

25. Scott Hamilton, director, Las Vegas Economic Development, and Romeo Betea, interviewed by Gerald L. Gordon, August 7, 2008.

26. Downs, *New Visions for Metropolitan America*.

27. "House of Cards—Las Vegas: Too Many People in the Wrong Place, Celebrating as a Way of Life," http://radicalurbantheory.com/davis/housecards.html, 4.

28. Pollack, "How We Got Here—A Triumph of Will: An Economic History of Greater Phoenix," 2.

29. Ibid., 4.

30. Bernard and Rice, *Sunbelt Cities*, 310.

31. Ibid., 312.

32. Breugmann, *Sprawl*, 20.

33. Worden and de Kok, "Population Growth in Arizona," 25.

34. Pollack, "How We Got Here," 4.

35. Markley, "A Framework for Develoing Rural Entrepreneurship," 1.

36. Henry and Drabenscott, "A New Micro View of the U.S. Rural Economy," 53.

37. Plosila, "Building Innovation-Driven Regional Economies."

38. "Lenoir County Economic Development Summit," 13.

39. Henry and Drabenscott, "A New Micro View of the Untied State Rural Economy," 67.

40. "Building the Rural Economy with High Growth Entrepreneurs," http://www.kc.frb/org: 60.

41. Bingham and Mier, *Theories of Economic Development*, 65.

42. Wells, "Smart Growth at the Frontier: Strategies and Resources for Rural Communities," 3.

43. Ibid., 4.

44. Olson, "Economic Change in Rural America," remarks to the Fergus Falls Rotary Club, Fergus Falls, Minnesota (2002).

45. McGranahan and Wojan, "The Creative Class: A Key to Rural Growth," http://iers. usda.gov/amberwaves/april07/features/creative.htm, 6.

46. National Governors Association, "The Role of Arts in Economic Development," 3.

47. Downs, *New Visions*, 53.

48. Henton et al., *Grass Roots Leaders,* 6.

49. Hevesi, "Smart Growth in New York State," 9.

50. Puget Sound Regional Council, "Economic Analysis of the Central Puget Sound Region," 136.

51. Porter, "The Competitive Advantage of the Inner City," 1.

52. Ibid., 2.

53. Cortright and Mayer, "Spinoffs, Startups, and Fast Growth Firms," 2.

54. Porter, "The Competitive Advantages of the Inner City," 12.

Chapter 6

Can Communities Suffer from Too Much Success?

6.1 Introduction

Communities that enjoy economic growth will almost certainly encounter what some in the community will see as less-than-desirable consequences of that growth. This may be congestion in schools or on the roads, higher taxes, or various environmental impacts. The questions for local decision makers are, of course, whether there are viable alternatives to such growth and at what point a balance between the benefits and drawbacks of growth is reached.

Different communities recognize different realities and must respond accordingly. For example, in Fairfax County, Virginia, because residential growth cannot be stopped and because residents cost more in public services than they contribute in taxes, and because nearly two-thirds of the local general fund comes from real estate taxes, it is clear that commercial growth must continue as long as residential growth continues. Commercial growth has, over the past twenty-five to thirty years, been a large part of the reason the local board of supervisors has been able to *reduce* the real estate tax rate by more than 35 percent while the population *increased* by more than 90 percent and the general fund increased nearly eightfold.

Despite the many benefits inherent in local economic growth, there are specific concerns. And there is sometimes an overriding concern that growth could diminish the very attractiveness that encouraged businesses to consider sites in the community in the first place. Smilor et al. wrote, in reference to Austin, Texas, that "the possibility that growth will diminish the very qualities that caused the area to be attractive to high technology companies in the first place. This fine balance between a sustained quality of life and sustained economic development has been evident…with each new economic development activity, there was likely to be some community group that felt that the loss of some, from their view central, aspect of Austin that made the city unique, desirable, and affordable."[1] Phoenix, too, suffered from concerns that its growth might destroy the very attractiveness that led to it. A few critics complained about the 'Los Angelization' of Phoenix and the 'Californication' of Arizona."[2]

This is not necessarily an irrational position. It is perhaps even self-evident that there will be some unintended consequences that result from local economic growth. The most obvious will be more people: more traffic on the roads, more children in the schools, more shoppers in the stores. To a point, this may be regarded as a positive, but at some point, not everyone will regard growth as beneficial. Of course, the optimum course for communities in growth mode is to take the best that such growth has to offer while minimizing any unwanted consequences.

6.2 Magnifying Existing Problems

We know that, in a growth economy, people and businesses have location options. For individuals, especially if they are well-trained or well-educated, one very big option is increased mobility. "Going forward, the most challenging competition faced by firms will be the competition for people—for human talent. Those regions that offer a high quality of life will be the winners in this competition."[3]

Of course, not all communities are focused on preserving an existing quality of life. Some are concerned with how best to market that quality of life to attract businesses and investors to the area. Congressman Tom Osborne noted that that is certainly true in rural communities and smaller towns across the country. Nebraska, he wrote, is "rich in quality education, affordable cost of living, quality health care, safe communities, and strong family values."[4] Again, the challenge for local elected and appointed officials, and the community at large, is to determine which alternatives work best for their local situations, where the best balance lies, and how best to pursue the needed economic growth while addressing the accompanying challenges.

Communities that are successful in growing the local or regional economies experience unintended impacts in a variety of ways. The result most frequently cited has to do with congestion, but there are other issues that arise from economic growth. The costs to the local government of providing public services will increase. As has already been argued, the tax contributions from businesses typically far outweigh the marginal costs of providing public services, but there will still be an increased level of service required in many areas of municipal budgets. This is a need that must be anticipated by the relevant local governments so that financial planning can be effective.

As business grows, new workers are attracted to the community. This can put a strain on housing markets if there is a current shortage of a variety of types of housing. Of course, this can also be a blessing for communities in which many houses are on the market and the market is depressed. For the former instance, there is no quick fix. If a company selects a location in which housing is not immediately available, there will, of course, be a lag time before builders can respond. The economic impact on the community of the construction will be a positive one, but options need to be put into place to house the workers in the interim period. A related effect of this situation will be in the area of pricing; increased demand, especially in a depressed market, can have an upward impact on prices.

Although many regions consider development in light of the pressures placed on roads and other man-made infrastructure, the greatest challenge for other areas is the demand placed on natural resources. Cities experiencing the dramatic growth that has been seen in Las Vegas and Phoenix must anticipate future demands for water and implement plans to provide increasing supplies as well as implement and enforce a range of conservation measures.

The population of Las Vegas doubled between 1990 and 2007. And 90 percent of the area's water is supplied by the Colorado River, which, according to Alex Hutchinson (*Popular Mechanics,* February 2007), is in the throes of the worst drought in recorded history. The water dams at Lake Mead, which, Anderson (*NuWire Investor,* November 6, 2007) reports, is at less than half its normal level. Solutions are being tested and new technologies are being devised, but many in the area continue to call for a moratorium on development.

Such actions, however, may create a conundrum. To limit development may create an increase in demand for housing and drive up prices. To permit development may overtax available resources and drive up the prices of those assets. A delicate balancing act is required. And these areas need to be careful not only about the resources themselves, but about their reputations as good places to live and work—both today and into the future.

Las Vegas businesses and residents are almost entirely dependent upon the reservoir at Lake Mead for their water supply. According to Reuters (*NuWire Investor,* November 6, 2007), it is the source of more than 90 percent of the area's water supply. Further, it was reported that the lake was about half full, in part due to the fact that the region's population had grown by about 50 percent in the previous eight years. The same article asserts that "investors should always remember that water flows toward money—it's no different from oil or electricity…The booming cities of the west will not run dry no matter how complex the water situation becomes."

Although this is a great attitude to have when working to attract businesses, it is perhaps overly optimistic. For the time being, this may not be an immediate issue, but surely at some point, regardless of the strength of the desire to provide water for developments, natural shortages will overwhelm the intent. Hutchinson (*Popular Mechanics,* February 2007) for example, reported that the Colorado River, the source of 90 percent of the water that supports life in Nevada. Many of the "solutions" that have been cited or are being tried have critics. Aquifers that are being developed may not have sufficient capacity to keep pace with the growing demand; new wells may cause problems for the surrounding land.

The Phoenix area has been working on the problem a bit longer and has a variety of projects under way and is seeking to develop a long-term supply under the most difficult circumstances. Their challenge is the same in another sense, however: businesses that may be attracted to the region must be convinced that the supplies are abundant today and will be available in the future, without significantly discomforting restrictions and at reasonable costs.

Some communities have concerns about more general environmental impacts of business growth. Construction of both the business facilities and workforce housing will use land and result in increased use of vehicles. This, in turn, results in more pollution from car exhausts, the lawn mowers of homeowners, and a variety of other environmental impacts. As well, communities that are experiencing growth of either the business or residential sectors need to ensure that there are adequate utilities to accommodate the growth. Expanding uses of electricity and water can cause shortages or raise the prices for existing users of those resources. Sewer and wastewater treatment facilities will also feel the strain of demands from new development if prior planning for expansions is not effective.

6.3 Addressing New Problems

Rapidly expanding employment opportunities in a given area can have the result of creating a sellers' market. Employers that have experienced difficulties in filling jobs generally, or positions requiring specific skill sets, may find that new employers to the community exacerbate the problem of finding employees and create a demand-driven rise in salary requirements. On the other hand, as has been discussed, communities that create and gain awareness of an industry cluster can use that strength to market the area for employees as well as businesses.

In the longer term, the competition for a relatively scarce workforce can be overcome by creating the mass of companies that constitute the cluster. This suggests two actions by local officials: develop and promote the industry cluster, and provide in the community the educational and training support for the development and retraining of the relevant workforces.

An additional concern that can grow in the face of economic growth relates to the use of the aforementioned economic development incentives. Resentment can result either because the incentive used to attract new businesses was taken from the state and local taxes paid by existing companies for years, or because the incoming businesses have been excused from paying taxes going forward while the longer-standing businesses are still required to pay their share. State and local decision makers need to assess these potential reactions very carefully before offering incentive packages.

6.4 Managing Local Expectations

Communities that become increasingly aggressive in the outreach for business attraction and economic growth, or that decide to grow businesses locally, will often confront a sense of rising expectations that employment opportunities and wealth generation are on the way. It becomes somewhat more difficult to sell a program that will build relationships and, over time, maybe result in businesses coming to the area or existing firms expanding significantly. But that is the reality: economic development requires time and patience. And that is a tougher sell for residents and even for elected officials. Thus, administrators need to exercise caution in not overselling the timing or magnitude of expected outcomes. And elected officials need to be similarly cautious in reporting plans to their constituents.

Incentive programs raise special needs for the management of local expectations. A white paper prepared for the U.S. Department of Commerce by the National Association of State Development Agencies (NASDA) reflects this challenge for participating local governments. "As more sophisticated monitoring and evaluation tools are implemented, economic developers will play an important role in managing expectations among stakeholders."[5] Will this rigor and diligence be enough to help control the reasonableness of local expectations by elected officials, residents, or the business community?

Often, regardless of how well delivered the voice of reason is in terms of expectations, communities can, over time, begin to wonder why results have not yet been realized or why the outcomes aren't greater. Clearly, a vital part of designing an economic development outreach effort is the development of a communications plan. Many communities do have plans to communicate with the business community externally, but not all have deliberate plans for communications internally. Economic development practitioners and local elected officials can derive numerous benefits from locally targeted communications outreach. Not only can it help to manage the expectations and reactions of the community, but it can also support the elected officials who have voted to spend relatively scarce resources on business attraction.

In a highly developed internal communications plan for economic growth, the message is carried by individuals in several areas of the community. Elected officials, economic development practitioners, private sector representatives, and community institutions (e.g., education, health care, and hospitality) can all make the pitch to residents. As long as the message points are consistent, the story can be told in a reinforcing and compelling way. In addition to consistent key message points, each of the contributors can make specific points. Elected officials can address the impacts on the community of economic growth, including the ability to provide more or better public services from an expanding tax base. Elected officials also have a role in the announcement of expansions or relocations and can use those opportunities to remind constituents of the plan and the progress being made against it. This, too, will help manage local expectations.

The private sector can also play a role in communicating with the community. Many of those whom such a plan is designed to reach will be their employees. Internal communiqués from the companies' leadership, newsletters, and even informal brown bag lunches are good ways to explain to some residents why business growth is important and what can be expected. One particularly positive message point for constituents from local businesses relates to the amount of purchases made from local vendors. This demonstrates that, as the area's economy expands, it can benefit many others in the community. The real keys to these kinds of communications efforts are for the messages to be accurate, concise, consistent, delivered by various sources, and delivered in a manner that does not appear to be "spin," but rather informational and educational.

In some communities, local governments have asked the business community to help finance the economic development program. This may work in some places, but not others. Where it has not been successful, there are a number of reasons, some of which are summarized as follows:

1. Private funds are even more susceptible to economic conditions than are public dollars. A period of economic slowdown is precisely the time that localities need to be *more* aggressive than ever about business attraction and retention; yet, it is also the very time that private funding sources would not be able to be supportive.
2. If groups are successful in soliciting private monies, presumably much of it would originate in the locality's most vital economic submarkets. It is very likely that those sources would be primarily interested in seeing the impacts of the expenditures centered in their vicinity only. This may be to the further detriment of those submarkets in greatest need.
3. A similar concern may relate to contributions from developers or land or facility owners who then might expect priority consideration of economic development prospect referrals to their sites or projects.
4. A large contribution to an economic development program from local businesses could result in an interest in exercising disproportionate control over the program. These programs should be consistent with the vision of the community's elected leadership, in concert with, but not necessarily driven by, the private sector.
5. Economic development is, at its heart, all about being able to provide for the economic well-being and the quality of life for the citizens of, workers in, and visitors to a community. This is a public responsibility.
6. Raising private capital is a professional exercise that, when done properly and effectively, generally costs as much as a third of the total generated to pay for the costs of the campaign. The end result will be more and more meetings under the general task of "investor relations." These may distract managers from the actual work of economic development.

7. Fund-raising by the local economic development program would also place them in direct competition with the fund-raising of other organizations, including those in support of the eradication and treatment of diseases, cultural groups and the arts, and other programs.

Community leaders need to address their economic development needs in concert with their business and residential communities. Great things can be accomplished over time, but the expectations of what can be done need to be clear, shared, and reconsidered carefully over time. Finally, such examinations need to be mindful of the enormous contributions the business community makes to the life of most communities that are not reflected in jobs, wealth, or tax revenues. Businesses are quite often excellent corporate citizens, contributing both time and money to community organizations and charitable good works. They do not do so for publicity reasons, but rather because they are part of the community and wish to give back in some way to the community that supports them and their employees. This was expressed succinctly by a senior executive of ExxonMobil who delivered the keynote address at the 2008 annual conference of the Virginia Chamber of Commerce:

> While it is the responsibility of the Commonwealth of Virginia to provide a business environment and infrastructure that provides companies with a competitive advantage to be successful, this relationship must be a partnership. It is our responsibility as businesses in Virginia to give back to the communities in which we operate. At ExxonMobil, we take our corporate responsibility very seriously. In Virginia alone, ExxonMobil employees volunteer thousands of hours of time and resources back to their communities. These activities range from providing individual tutoring in English, math, and science at local elementary schools, to cleaning up the Potomac River shores. From supporting the INOVA blood drives to building homes with Habitat for Humanity.[6]

As was also stated relative to the role that Boeing plays in the life of the Seattle region, communities are extremely fortunate to have such vital and engaged employers in their areas.

Notes

1. "The Austin/San Antonio Corridor: The Dynamics of a Developing Technopolis," http://www.utexas.edu/depts/ic2/pubs/corr, 22.
2. Bernard and Rice, *Sunbelt Cities*, 321.
3. Puget Sound Regional Council, "Economic Analysis of the Central Puget Sound Region," 106.
4. Osborne, "Revitalizing Rural Nebraska," *Rural Economic Development Handbook*, 4.

5. National Association of State Development Agencies, "Evaluating Business Development Incentives," viii.

6. Hal Cramer, president, Fuels Marketing Division, ExxonMobil, "Thirty Years in Virginia: What We've Learned," presentation to the Virginia Chamber of Commerce, October 29, 2008.

Chapter 7

Will the Formula Change?: Community Economic Growth in the Second Decade of the Millennium

7.1 The Growth Industries of Tomorrow

The industries that will drive economic growth in the future may be variations on the themes of the industries of today. New technologies will enable things to be done faster, cheaper, more frequently, and perhaps with less labor. Energy will still need to be generated and transmitted to the consumer, but the sources of energy may be renewable as well as the oil, gas, and coal extractions of today, and the transmission may include higher speeds and more efficient methods. Indeed, power may even be stored in fuel cells and then shipped to the consumer.

Much has been written about the effects of global warming and the need to develop new and innovative means of conservation as well as technologies both to conserve energy and to provide resources to supplant the use of nonrenewable supplies. This could be the greatest challenge mankind will have to face in the coming decades. With all such problems, researchers swing into action to seek solutions and the business community becomes motivated to develop, perfect, and market those solutions. And those businesses will create jobs that will need to be located in offices and labs, and perhaps even in fields and warehouses.

One of the encouraging things about the jobs that will evolve around green technologies and alternative energy sources is that, although there may be some concentrations of research and development, the implementation will be universal. That means that there could be opportunities for economic growth in regions, cities, and small towns throughout the United States. It is yet to be made clear what the full nature of the jobs or the facilities will be, so communities that wish to share in this growth need to keep an eye on developments in these fields and evaluate what assets will be required to attract the jobs and to grow the companies involved. And, as with any industry, where those assets are not present, local leaders may wish to consider how best to acquire them.

In the short-term future, it is not the industry sectors that will change. Change will come in the conception, testing, and practical applications of new methods. This means that communities will probably be able to base continued business attraction and economic growth in general by acquiring and applying the new technologies that will enable their businesses to be more competitive. From the perspective of the communities, that will enable them to seize the future comparative advantages that will enable them to be successful in economic development.

The intersection of today's technologies will also generate new directions for technology business growth. "Biotech today is an infant industry...Advances in and cooperation among biotechnology, information technology, and nanotechnology give rise to new developments and dimensions related to life sciences...rapid economic growth has generally been the outcome of complex interplay between a collection of largely unanticipated discoveries clumping and clustering in different fields over not a couple of months or even years, but decades."[1]

These new technologies will increase performance in many goods-producing and service-providing industries. By creating greater efficiencies, advanced technologies may also have the effect of eliminating jobs. Local economies based heavily on the types of employers that will be able to replace people with equipment will have a challenge. On the other hand, new technologies often create different kinds of jobs. The personal computer probably resulted in the loss of many administrative jobs in the business world, but also created opportunities for manufacturing and software development and more.

The U.S. Department of Labor's Bureau of Labor Statistics notes that many existing industries and job categories will continue to grow in the future. Specifically cited in the report are the following: service provision, education and health services, health care and social assistance, professional and business services, employment in scientific research and services, leisure and hospitality, construction trades, and government. Great emphasis is placed throughout the report on the growth of various health care occupations.[2]

In short, many of the high growth industries of the future will be those that require creative talent, thought processes, and service provision that is immediately proximate to the client or consumer. The development and application of new technologies as well as service sector employment will help drive local economic growth in the future. Some communities may have the assets that will draw and retain such employers and individuals.

Communities that have an existing competitive advantage can build upon that, but need to be ever mindful of the changes expected in the manner of production or service provision. Those who can do so effectively will keep the advantage. Those who find themselves with obsolete methods will lose their attractiveness to industry. This may mean that the localities that house the people and facilities actually developing the technologies may have an edge over those awaiting transfers. Additional research and development from within businesses, universities, institutes, government laboratories, and individuals will often also take place in proximity to the location of the original discovery. Some of the original work to develop the protocols for DARPA that initially led to the DARPAnet and then ultimately resulted in the evolution of the Internet took place in Reston, Virginia. It is therefore no mystery that companies like America Online, UUNet, PSINet, Network Solutions, and many more grew throughout the nearby region, creating tens of thousands of jobs and enormous wealth.

Communities can hope to spark the development of business technologies in numerous ways. We have already seen how the creative class of workers may be drawn to an area by a creative environment. They will also be attracted by the presence of opportunities to conduct research and to access college and university resources, human and machine, to further their investigations. A municipal regulatory structure that encourages experimentation and the commercialization of the output will also be attractive to those with an entrepreneurial spirit and will encourage those in the community to explore their own innovativeness.

The proximity of sources of venture capital and angel investors will also enable the growth of technologies in a region. Many companies have moved from one area to another to be close to the source of the capital that would be invested in the research and development phases of new technologies. Public agencies also have programs that can provide support while developing a new product. Once the technology results in a company or companies being born, the host site will have a clear competitive advantage in that sector.

Localities have often found that incubator programs have a great impact on the development of new technologies as well as creating new businesses using existing technologies. These incubators allow nascent businesses to access shared facilities and business services in a common location. By reducing the costs of starting the business, individuals can devote their full attention to the development of the technology. There are many models for business incubators and there exists a wealth of resources and guidance available for incubator programs from the National Business Incubator Association.

Clearly, the evolution of technologies and the new industries, companies, and jobs that they spawn enlarges the role of a community's colleges and universities.

These institutions have a stake in the growth of a community's commercial base. And they can play important roles in the attraction and retention of employers through training, retraining, research and development, and various contributions to the local quality of life. It is no coincidence that the case examples used in this book to demonstrate a range of lessons include communities in which a strong university or college plays an active role in economic development: Austin (the University of Texas); the Silicon Valley (Stanford); Fairfax County, Virginia (George Mason University); Pittsburgh (Carnegie-Mellon); and others.

Many of these means of supporting the creation of the innovation that can help lead to new companies, new jobs, and a stable economic future can be implemented in most communities. The lesson for localities is to put into place the structure and assets that will encourage the development and evolution of innovation and creative companies.

7.2 The Changing Components of Site Location Decisions

The traditional mantra for site location decision makers was "location, location, location." Companies needed to be in close proximity to suppliers or customers or transportation networks. Some of that still remains the case, but much of it changed with the advance of information technology and telecommunications technology. There are, of course, businesses that still need to be near customers or natural resources or other inputs, but, in many cases, the businesses no longer need to be close to the customer and employees don't need to be near the office.

In the case of businesses for which "location, location, location" is a passé bromide, a wide range of locations becomes possible. What, then, sets one apart from the other? What gives one community the comparative advantage that so many are seeking? The answers lie in what the targeted industries and companies need to succeed and what the decision makers need to be happy in a community. To a very great extent, these are factors that local officials cannot control. Some people prefer an urban setting or a more peaceful, rural lifestyle. For some, there will be a need to be close to a major customer or research facility. Some site location decisions are based on where a relative lives or where one's children reside.

Because several key decision-making factors may be out of control for the local community, it becomes increasingly important for communities to manage what can be controlled. Strategies may include the improvement of schools' performance, the beautification of main streets or industrial sites, improved telecommunications or transportation infrastructure, the provision of a variety of support services, or the regulatory environment. It is the elements of the site location decision-making process that communities can control that will define the economic development strategy. Two critical components of the controllable factors will pertain to workforce and the quality of life in the community.

Businesses absolutely require a reliable and abundant workforce that is trained in the areas of technology that they will apply. Further, the labor pool that demonstrates the capacity for keeping pace with new technology as it emerges will be a valuable asset for any business. From the perspective of the community, this means not only workers who are skilled and capable of acquiring additional skills, but it also means that the community being considered for a facility or office has the institutions available to provide the training regularly to upgrade skills. Whether this is a trade school, college, or university, the institution must also have a history of interaction with the local business community to ensure that the course offerings are current and available at times and places that are convenient to full-time employees.

Quality-of-life factors are, of course, much more ephemeral. What is important to one person may be less so or not important at all to others. There will be, however, some that are universal to all site location decisions. The first is public safety: no business will want to locate, or remain, in a community that is unsafe. A safe neighborhood means less expense is incurred for security and that the recruitment of employees will be easier. A second common quality-of-life factor is the quality of the public education system. Employers do not want to incur the additional costs of private education for their children. And even the senior executives, who might be able to afford private schools for their children, will be concerned that the people they want to employ may not. This is a comment that is heard regularly from executives in technology companies. The young men and women they want to attract to work for them have had the benefit of strong educations themselves and they expect the same for their children.

Colleges and universities play a similar role. Colleges and universities contribute to a community's ongoing economic growth not only through the preparation of a labor force, the provision of retraining, and research and development, and the transfer of technology-to-invention-to-commercialization. Campuses are typically large landholders that may pay significant sums in local taxes. They have concert halls and special event venues as well as ball fields and public events. Students and faculty purchase goods and services in the community and visitors to the area create business for local hotels, restaurants, and more.

It would be inaccurate to characterize the site location decision-making process as mechanical and data-driven. Companies will not only be interested in the location and the labor force, but will also be drawn to different lifestyles in different communities. They will also be attracted by what is sometimes referred to as the "buzz" that is attributed to exciting communities and vibrant economies. Quite often, businesses are retained in a community because they feel valued by others. Of course, the reverse of that statement is also a truism.

These intangible qualities frequently play a significant role in business attraction and retention. Localities with an attractive range of outdoor or cultural opportunities may have an appeal to decision makers that exceeds mere dollars and cents considerations. It is also clear that these factors can only make an impact on executives and their advisors if they have visited a place. For this reason, economic development programs are often linked closely to their convention and visitor agency counterparts. If an executive visits an area—for whatever reason—and has a positive experience, there is a greatly enhanced likelihood that he or she will make a positive site location decision for that community if the situation arises. Putting a community's "best foot forward" to tourists, meeting attendees, vacationers, parents visiting children at college, and others can have an impact on the future economic growth of the locality.

There is also a growing awareness that communities can actually create these amenities and make them more attractive as business locations. Such amenities attract the types of talented workers needed by today's businesses. National Public Radio's "Marketplace" correspondent Chris Farrell said it well: "making it easier to turn warehouses into dance studio space or encouraging the growth of theater in your area and…making the regulations and the zoning more supportive" can be very appealing to young, creative workers.

A 2001 article by the National Governors Association further notes that "arts programs have served as components of high-impact economic development programs by assisting state and local government in the following ways:

- Leveraging human capital and cultural resources to generate economic vitality in underperforming regions
- Restoring and revitalizing communities by serving as a centerpiece for downtown redevelopment
- Creating vibrant public spaces integrated with natural amenities, resulting in improved urban quality of life, an expanded business and tax revenue base, and a positive regional and community image
- Contributing to a region's "innovation habitat" by…making communities more attractive to highly desirable, knowledge-based employees, and permitting new forms of knowledge-intensive production to flourish"[3]

The same report notes that local governments can play a role in facilitating such growth: "Government-led efforts have catalyzed private development interest in the adaptive reuse of urban structures to create retail, residential, commercial, and cultural spaces. As these projects gain momentum, additional private capital has flowed into the areas surrounding these projects."[4] Once again, these controllable factors can provide community leaders with a road map of strategies to address when trying to establish stable economic growth for the future.

7.3 Diversification of the Local Economic Base

It has been observed all too often that a local economy that is overly dependent upon a single industry or a single company, no matter how invincible it may seem at present, opens itself to the peaks and valleys of the macro-economic scene or, at a minimum, an inconsistent demand for products over time. It has been discussed here in the case studies of Seattle (Boeing), Pittsburgh (steel), Fairfax County (government and government contracting), and Houston (oil). In other areas that were similarly overdependent on a single industry, foreign competition with its comparative advantage of lower wage rates has caused disruption of regional economies and devastated entire communities. Consider the textile industry of New England or even the outsourcing of technology services to India.

Given the current state of affairs in various sectors of the financial industry, one might imagine the importance of a diversified economic base to officials in New York, Charlotte, and other large banking centers. Local economies that are based on more than one pillar are inherently more stable. Communities that have enjoyed long-term growth and stability are those that have several pillars supporting the local economy. And often, these industry sectors will be vastly different in nature: manufacturing and business-to-business services, personal services and tourism, or software and biotech. Another form of diversity is that which is found within a general industry. For example, telecommunications may be the broad basis of a local economy, but that may include research and design, testing, manufacturing, software production, or sales and service. And the diversification of various segments of the oil industry was cited as a stabilizing factor in the Houston economy, although even Houston did have one brief period during which the faltering of their single industry dominance resulted in a difficult time for the region.

Consider the localities noted earlier: Seattle, Pittsburgh, Fairfax County, and Houston. Seattle's economy, from the early 1970s, fluctuated wildly as it reflected its dominant employer, the Boeing Corporation. As the Puget Sound region emerged from a series of economic rises and falls, it planned an economy constructed on a base of several diversified industry sectors. Today, aerospace is complemented by a strong information technology sector and a vibrant biotechnology cluster. This recently emerged diversification of the economic base has enabled the entire region to smooth out its economic output, its employment base, and its general quality of life.

Similarly, Pittsburgh, when it emerged from the doldrums of having lost its steel-based economic future, pursued a policy of diversified growth. No longer would a single industry or a single employer dominate the region's economic and political landscapes. Today, Pittsburgh is a cultural, medical, and academic center.

In Fairfax County, the economic base had once been dominated by the largest employer in the greater Washington, D.C., region: the federal government. Those who did not work directly for the federal government worked for companies that contracted their services to the Department of Defense and other federal agencies. Each time an administration mentioned cost-saving reductions in the federal workforce or savings in federal procurement, the entire region took a deep breath. Today, the private sector dominates employment in Fairfax County, with strengths in information technology, aerospace technology, biotechnology, telecommunications, minority businesses, and foreign-owned companies. This diversity of industry has meant that only once in the past twenty-five years has the county experienced a net job loss.

Houston, as has been noted, is a somewhat different case. Although new industry clusters—medical, for example—have grown to replace an economy once based solely on oil companies, the oil business is still predominant. The advantage to Houston is that the oil business has numerous facets to it and those are each represented within the region, giving it a diversity within the industry.

In each case, the lesson learned is clear. Economies that are overly dependent upon a single industry or a singly major employer are likely to be subject to sharp and even unexpected downward trends as the industry in question is buffeted by factors outside the ability of anyone local to control. Control has come through an economic diversification that allows the misfortunes of one industry or one employer to be absorbed by the growth and stability of other employers and other industry sectors.

7.4 The Economics of Inclusion

Communities throughout the United States are encountering increasing levels of diversity in their neighborhoods, schools, and businesses. This can clearly bring challenges for localities. The costs of public services for a growing population can be daunting when there is complete homogeneity among the newcomers and the existing residents. However, the costs of providing public services are usually exacerbated by an influx of people for whom English is not the primary language. Consider, as an example, Fairfax County, where 38 percent of all children have at least one parent who was not born in the United States, and where one public elementary school has nearly 250 tongues and dialects in the same school. Imagine the increased costs involved in providing public education in the context of so many different languages and cultures. And the same impacts are felt in providing police and fire services, human services, or even services at the public libraries and parks.

However, it is no coincidence that Fairfax County can also boast of what *Time* magazine called "one of the great economic success stories of our time" (*Time*, February 19, 2007). One focus group after another has identified ethnic diversity as an element that makes the county such a great place in which to live, work, and raise a family. In the neighborhoods, diversity makes life more interesting; in business, diversity brings a variety of perspectives, training, and viewpoints. It is likely that few business challenges can be resolved through the application of single solutions. Having different ways of viewing problems usually results in a range of feasible solutions, the optimum one not necessarily being the one that was "home grown."

Minority-owned businesses represent the largest category of business growth in recent years. As such, this segment of local economic growth may represent one of the greatest opportunities. In 2000, U.S. Commerce Secretary Mineta wrote that "minority-owned firms are surpassing the growth of all U.S. businesses, growing at a rate of 17% per year, six times the growth rate of all firms."[5] Localities can abet this process by providing connections, business finance, and training to enable these businesses to grow locally.

Richard Florida spoke of tolerance as another of the key features of the creative economy. But that stops a half step short of one clear reality: merely being accepting of people from different cultures is a half step. The communities of the future will be those that reflect the American "melting pot" of the big cities of the past century. Here is the string of logic: local economies will benefit from having people from different cultures being part of the business community; people from around the world who look at the United States will consider a variety of factors when choosing a community in which to settle; communities will, in the future if not already, be competing for this commercial asset just like they do for any other commercial asset, and just as they do for the best and brightest American-born workers.

Men and women from other countries will select a place to live by asking themselves the same questions that Americans ask themselves, plus some: Do I know someone there? Are there jobs there for me, my spouse, and for my children when they reach working age? Are the schools good? But they will also ask other questions: Are there other people from my country in the community? How have they been received? Are there places of worship and groceries that suit my needs?

The technology businesses of today that will populate the business landscape of tomorrow do not care whether their employees are white or black or Asian or Latino or other. They only care that they are well-trained, trainable, hard-working, and smart. In fact, my guess is that the most successful technology companies of our time not only recognize the virtue of openness, but also insist on a profile that announces their openness to the world, their clients, potential clients, and future workers.

All things being equal, it is an absolute guarantee that workers coming to the United States will only consider those communities about which they have some knowledge! Because they will not be likely to entertain unknown possibilities, it becomes incumbent upon the communities that are interested in attracting these men and women to make known their interest, the business opportunities that exist, and the amenities they possess. The clearest example of this, to date, has been in the high-technology areas where the demand for a trained workforce has often been so great that internal (U.S.) supply has been greatly inadequate. The inability to accept or perform work, thus dampening profits, has often been cited as hindrance to the growth of local economies. Given that great numbers of IT workers, with fluency in English, are foreign-born, the ability to attract them is as important today as "location, location, location" was in the past. Again, communities will be competing for this relatively scarce and valuable business resource like they compete for any other such resource, and must be assertive and constant in their efforts to attract it.

7.5 Funding Local Economic Development: The Twin Pillars of Sufficiency and Consistency

One of the classic definitions of politics has to do with the allocation of scarce resources over legitimate, competing demands. Local elected officials are thus confronted with the question of how aggressive to be when funding economic development programs at times when more teachers or firefighters are needed, or various essential public works are required. Unlike many other public service line items, economic development can be accurately characterized as an investment in the future of the community. It is a current expenditure that will enable elected officials to build the economy that will deliver the funds at some future date that will enable the provision of more and better public schools and other public services. This leaves elected officials with decisions to make regarding the resolution of today's problems or the longer-term picture.

The cynic says that local elected officials will first address the short-term issues because they need the votes to be re-elected. I would argue that most elected officials have a sincere desire to establish the type of economic stability that will provide funding for those needs well into the future. Most will recognize that a stable economy and lower unemployment rates are usually consistent with better school performance, lower crime rates, and other improvements in the social conditions of communities.

It is how the relative needs of present and future challenges are viewed that leads communities to a balance in the level of investment in economic development programs relative to other public service needs. It is clear, in any case, that for economic development to be maximally effective, it must be funded at a level that is sufficient to reach the business decision makers in the identified industries. And it must be sufficiently funded over a long period of time to permit the establishment of community image and resource availability that will result in consideration for future sites, offices, and facilities.

However, sufficiency of funding alone will not be adequate to support local economic development efforts. Consistency is also key. This has two implications: the consistency of the level of effort that has already been addressed, and the consistency between the messages being sent and the reality of the community. It is one thing for a community to claim that it is "pro-business," but another thing entirely actually to be pro-business. Business site location decision making is today an art form that is practiced by in-house real estate and facilities professionals as well as external legal and location counselors. These are skilled men and women who often have as much information at their fingertips as do local officials. School results, demographic information, even costs of land and buildings in the community are today readily available and often public information. It is a given that the decisions will be extremely well-informed and there will be no surprises. Communities must not only promote themselves as being good places to do business; they must actually *be* good places to do business.

One of the concerns often heard by economic development professionals relates to the consistency of the pro-business environment over time. Companies do not want to locate where either state or local support and tax and regulatory environments change with administrations or are subject to review should Democrats or Republicans come into power. They look for consistency of political message and reality over the course of time, party, and administration at both the state and local levels.

7.6 Concluding Thoughts

The formula for local economic growth has clearly changed. Manufacturing is not the large employer it once was; neither is farming. U.S. employment in these sectors has been replaced by foreign competition and the forces of technology. Advances in nanotechnology will some day accelerate the pace of that change. How will this impact our communities?

The one constant in the formula for economic growth in the future will be rapid change. Moving forward, changes in site location decision factors will change as frequently as businesses themselves, or their inherent technologies change. And the pace of this change is likely to increase at an increasing rate.

Communities will be best able to sustain their local economies through such changes if they are home to more fully diversified economic bases. As change impacts one technology or one company, or even an entire industry, stability in other sectors will help to sustain the local economy and the tax base that supports the quality of life in the community.

What makes a community a good place for companies is no longer essentially its physical location. Capital availability, community institutions, and quality-of-life features are now more vital than ever. As congested areas find their lifestyles threatened, alternative locations become increasingly attractive to employers. Geographic locational factors will again be paramount for sectors such as technology-based manufacturing, storage and distribution, and various value-added functions. We are already seeing this with the advent of foreign automobile manufacturing in the United States to have the finished products be closer to American markets.

Given the evolution of technology—particularly in communications—the economic growth of the future will seek out locations that can provide cost advantages, qualified labor pools, institutions for training and retraining at all levels, and attractive lifestyle options for everyone.

The communities whose pursuits of growth will be the most successful will be those that both possess these amenities and that can most effectively communicate their benefits to the relevant audiences consistently over time.

Notes

1. Bruce Felps, "Biotech, Infotech, Nanotech Poised to Alter 21st Century Economies," http://www.masshightech.com/stories/2002/04/story81, 1.
2. Bureau of Labor Statistics, http://www.bls.gov/oco/oco2003.htm.
3. National Governors Association, "The Role of Arts in Economic Development," 1.
4. Ibid., 3.
5. Mineta, "The Minority Business Challenge," iii.

Chapter 8

Conclusions

8.1 Introduction

Economic growth can take many different forms. The form that it takes in any given community is a function of the assets, resources, and geographic considerations of the area in question as well as the intentions, plans, and effectiveness of the local leaders. Given the resources that exist as well as those that can be developed, economic development may mean business attraction in one community and office park development in another. It can mean infrastructure improvements in one town and tourism promotion in the next. It may focus on job development or employer retention or wealth creation or trade enhancement.

Economic growth in a community must be designed to raise the conditions of all people and all businesses in a community. There is a double loss if groups are left behind as the community grows. The creation or extension of an economic underclass that is not part of the economic advance means that the community is not gaining growth at the maximum possible rate because it has excluded a portion of its assets from the larger effort. At the same time, it has created a set of individuals who require support from those whose fortunes have advanced and who now must contribute, through taxes at a minimum, to the care of others. This means the expenditure of wealth on taxes rather than investment or the purchase of goods and services that yields several additional iterations of spending in the community.

For communities to grow, their businesses must grow. Michael Porter, in his seminal work on competitive strategy, describes the barriers to entry for businesses. The same factors may be considered by localities when pursuing programs of business attraction and retention. Porter defines economies of scale as "declines in the unit's cost of production."[1] This is applicable to a community because business site location decision makers will locate where the costs of operating are advantageous.

Porter's other factors have similar relevance. Communities must differentiate themselves from others to be competitive, just as products must be differentiated. There are various capital requirements that can be expected when operating in various locations, just as there are costs inherent in relocating or expanding operations within other communities. These are referred to as "switching costs" in Porter's lexicon.[2] Other factors, including cost disadvantages independent of economies of scale and access to distribution channels, also bear consideration at the community level.

Porter's final characteristic is governmental policy. This relates to policies implemented by the local government that affect the conduct of business (e.g., taxes, regulations, and processes). In reality, local governments can do much to grow their economies or, conversely, to constrain them. Local governments must be full partners with business to drive economic growth in the community. They must be proactive and aggressive, and they must provide the environment businesses require.

This book is a demonstration that local governments, with the strategic partnerships in their communities, can indeed influence the pace of economic growth. Further, there is abundant evidence that economic growth at the local level has benefits that are pervasive throughout the community. Many of the case studies considered herein illustrate how economic growth can yield communities that are not only good places to work, but that are highly livable as well. These are the communities whose main streets have found their own formula for economic growth.

8.2 The Historical Context for This Book

The Formula for Economic Growth on Main Street America was written and published in late 2008 and early 2009. The timing for the discussion of these topics has colored both the writing and the manner in which it will be received. The global and national economic environments of late 2008 were as dire as have been seen for decades; in some ways, for generations. Several large, marquee businesses have met their demise while others are struggling to stay afloat.

Entire industries have declined and many of the businesses that have pleaded with the government for years not to interfere have now approached Congress to bail them out. As has been discussed in this book, it is not a time to be involved in a local economy that is overly dependent upon a single business or industry cluster. Anyone who is unclear on that point need only ask the people of Detroit. Ford, General Motors, and Chrysler have made the argument that their industry and their companies should be bailed out by the federal government because of the potential negative consequences for their employees, their suppliers, and the entire Great Lakes region. After all, if the automobile industry falters, the industry base is not sufficiently diversified to support the region and the other clusters in the region are not sufficient to absorb the workforce. This is Boeing in the 1970s, or Pittsburgh and steel all over again.

Now the automobile industry is in the economic spotlight. Financial services firms are also seeking solutions and alternatives to going out of business. Banks are being bought and sold while Fannie Mae and others look for short-survival and long-term solutions. The Stock Market is breaking records for precipitous declines while public, corporate, and personal investments around the world are in something approaching free fall. And in the same way that all politics is local, all economic issues can be said to be local. As the national unemployment rate climbs, cities, towns, and regions throughout the United States are feeling the impact of the general business slowdown. As joblessness rises, the need for local governments to provide more services grows. More human services are needed to assist those who have lost their jobs; more family services may be needed for their children. There is typically a direct relationship between crime and the unemployment rate. When more people are out of work, various crime rates go up. These may be times when police and fire protection are more critical than ever. These are the times when local governments may need to enhance their provision of public services in a wide range of areas.

If a "perfect storm" is the confluence of several factors at the same time that combine to worsen individual problems exponentially, then late 2008–early 2009 could be seen as a perfect storm for localities and for local economies. An increasing demand for public services, a diminishment of revenues from public investments, and declining tax revenues resulting from lower employment levels have all combined to create tremendous pressures on local budgets.

Because businesses generally contribute more revenues to local tax bases than they take back in public services, business revenues can help to offset the cost of public services for residents and can be the savior of local economies and local government budgets. But in late 2008–early 2009, business generally was in decline and contributing less to local budgets to help with the provision of public services.

Local governments have reacted with employee furloughs, position freezes, layoffs, and program cuts. Again, at the very time that more people need more services, the funding is just not available to local decision makers. And because business is in a general decline, any contributions from the private sector to the local charitable organizations that might otherwise help provide human or health services are also in decline. In fact, such external sponsorships and contributions are typically the first items to be cut from budgets when the private sector begins to feel the pinch.

This perfect storm hit America's cities, counties, and regions hard. Although a relative few may have escaped the worst of the impacts, it is safe to say that only some have fared better than others. One has to wonder, then, what gave some communities an edge. The following statement opens this book: "It is not always evident why economic growth takes root in one area rather than another. Even within a single region, some communities may outpace their neighbors in securing the economic growth that leads to an enhanced quality of life." It is now time to wonder whether something can be said about why some communities are better able to withstand the national and even global economic problems and trends.

The following section will discuss the lessons that have been extracted from the case studies examined in this book. Perhaps these lessons can assist the thinking of communities as they try to recover and rebuild their economies so any problems experienced in future economic downcycles will have less impact. The short answer is preparation, diversification, and long-term investments in the development of the local economic base.

There is one final comment regarding general reactions to periods of serious economic problems: it has to do with human nature. When the economy falters, there tends to be less debate about slow growth or no-growth; suddenly, economic growth becomes more acceptable. There is an old joke that suggests that a recession is when your neighbor is unemployed and a depression is when you are unemployed. In truth, when the various components of the perfect economic storm of late 2008–early 2009 began to be felt, the growth debate in many communities was tabled.

The first overall lesson in this is that local governments cannot afford to stop all growth and not all growth is bad (or good, for that matter). The second is that growing the local economy cannot be as effective when started in the depths of a recession. It needs to have been a long-standing policy of the local government that sustains the community through the bad times.

Strong economies of Main Street America are the result of long-term investments in the diversification and steady growth of what communities have determined they want and for which they have the requisite business assets.

So, what are the lessons learned from this review? The eight primary conclusions follow.

1. *Communities cannot allow themselves to become complacent.* Economic stability can be lost. One of my board members is fond of saying that "there is no divine right to prosperity." The proof behind that statement could have been found in 1960s Pittsburgh, 1970s Seattle, 1980s Long Island, or 1980s Houston. Steel, Boeing, Grumman, and the oil industry were all respectively perceived to be long-term sources of local economic stability and growth. In their respective recoveries, each emphasized economic diversity and quality-of-life amenities to support their comebacks; each incorporated economic development planning into their larger community comprehensive planning; and each found the necessary visionary leadership to light the right paths.

2. *A community cannot wait until the situation is dire to develop or further develop the economic base to carry it through the difficult times. The foundation must be laid when the national, global, and regional economies are strong; only then can it be sustained through downcycles in the economy.* Enough said.

3. *In a changing global economic paradigm, change is assured and must be embraced.* As technology changes and the very nature of our communities and regions changes, the business of business attraction and retention will also change. Localities that best comprehend, anticipate, and prepare for these changes will be the ones that are the most successful in courting employers and providing

for future economic stability. Part of what constitutes change is the changing demographic composition of this country and its communities. It is no longer sufficient merely to accept this change; it must be embraced. Economic growth will come fastest to the communities where everyone is involved in generating commerce, testing their entrepreneurial fortunes, and benefitting from the outcomes of economic growth.

4. *Communities must prepare for businesses as if dressing up for the big dance.* Many communities may, in any given situation, be courting the same business growth. One's appearance can make it a more attractive suitor than the other localities seeking expansions and relocations. That attractiveness must consist not only of business-related factors, but of quality-of-life features as well. As technologies advance, notably in the area of communications, quality-of-life factors will become increasingly critical. These include the physical environment, educational institutions, arts and cultural opportunities, and a general openness in the community to people of all races, origins, and backgrounds. It further implies safe and clean neighborhoods for families and individuals. A 2001 article by the National Governors Association lays out several tactics communities can use to "advance the integration of arts in economic development":
   - Encourage collaboration among the business community, state arts agencies, economic development, tourism and education
   - Evaluate and nurture culturally based industries indigenous to the state
   - Focus on changing regional and community images
   - Stay informed of innovation concerning the arts on the local level[3]

5. *Local governments—in both conscious and subconscious ways—influence the course of local economic growth.* "Effective leadership" is a term that has both general parameters and traits that are specific to the individual, those being led, and the time and place. One of the commonalities of local political leadership in the future will be the ability to foresee the community's economic needs, to plan its responses to environmental factors—both opportunities and threats—and to marshal the necessary resources to achieve the best future with the greatest benefits from economic growth with the minimal negative consequences. This does not apply only to a community's public officials, but to its corporate base as well. For example, the seven commissioners of the Fairfax County (Virginia) Economic Development Authority constitute its governing body. These are men and women whose business acumen and connections help drive planning and economic growth in one of the nation's strongest markets. Their sense of business operations and changes in the business community have been vital components of the programs of business attraction and retention in Fairfax County.

6. *Change, as it affects local economic growth, can be anticipated, and local expectations can be managed.* Strategic planning can enable a community to foresee

future needs and opportunities, and can outline the path to pursue to achieve the community's vision. However, seeing and doing are two different things. Communities must take a long-term approach to economic growth. They must allocate the necessary resources to be aggressive, to be competitive in an increasingly competitive business. Economic development programs should be seen as investments—from which returns can be expected—not simply as costs. And in especially difficult economic times, these efforts should be increased, not reduced. Following this course will, over time, produce results and improve life for both the businesses and residents of a community.

7. *Local governments neither have to prepare for, nor carry out plans for, local economic growth alone.* The communities that have most successfully driven economic growth are those that have approached both the planning and the implementation phases in tandem with a myriad of strategic partners in the community. The involvement and support of local strategic partners can either be broad and comprehensive or specifically inclusive of individuals and institutions relevant to the issues and needs of the community in question. Although not intended to be an exhaustive list, some of the potential strategic partnerships for communities are illustrated next:

Issue	Category	Strategic Partners
Broad leadership	Elected officials	State representatives
		Local elected officials
		Elected officials from neighboring jurisdictions
		School board members
	Appointed officials	City/county administrators
		School administrators
Community leadership	Citizens	Civic associations
		PTAs
		Military bases
Business growth	Business leadership	Chambers of commerce
		Technology councils
		Leadership organizations
		Industry associations
		Union representatives
		Regional business groups

Labor force	Education and training	Colleges and universities
		Trade and technical schools
		Private schools
		Workforce boards
Demographic	Diversity	Local government
		Demographers
		Faculty demographic experts
		Representatives of ethnic groups
Development	Land use and comprehensive planning	Local government staff
	Transportation	Relevant state staffs
	Environmental	Staffs of neighboring jurisdictions
	Public works	Builders' associations
	Open spaces	Advisory boards and commissions
	Housing	Airport management
Other quality-of-life factors	Arts and culture	Arts councils
	Hospitality	Arts organizations
		Convention and visitor bureaus
		Museums, attractions
		Developers
		Hoteliers
		Restaurateurs
		Owners of meeting space
		Travel agencies

Any who are unclear about the willingness of the business community to be involved as full partners in the communities in which they reside simply need to talk to senior business executives. The president of ExxonMobil's Fuels Marketing Division told the 2008 annual meeting of the Virginia Chamber of Commerce that "there is no greater testament to the attractiveness of our community than when our own children elect to stay in Virginia to work and raise their own families, as my two children and four grandchildren have done. Virginia provides an exceptional environment to raise families, to become active in the community, and to retire. In fact, ExxonMobil has nearly two thousand retirees that live in the Commonwealth, almost all of whom were originally from other states and countries. That truly speaks to the quality of life here in Virginia."[4] And that truly speaks to the interest of business to be fully engaged partners in the lives of the communities they call home. The value of such partnerships is immeasurable!

8. *Local economic growth can be achieved.* This book contains two types of case studies: communities whose economies collapsed and needed to be resuscitated and communities that experienced such extraordinarily rapid growth that they had to plan and make changes quickly to accommodate it. In both cases, the key lesson learned about the achievement of economic growth on Main Street America is that *it can be done*!

8.3 Afterword

The title of this book is *The Formula for Economic Growth on Main Street America*. Can there really be a formula that can be universally used and achieve results if properly applied?

Of course not. The definition of a formula is "a general fact, rule, or principle." An alternative definition from *Merriam-Webster* online is "a conventional statement intended to express some fundamental truth or principal."

There is no set formula that is fact. There is no specific or fundamental truth that must be applied or success will be fleeting. There exist only theories, indicators, and that which has often worked elsewhere. If, then, there exists no set formula, let's call the lessons identified herein a construct. A construct is defined by *Merriam-Webster* online as "a theoretical entity" or "a product of ideology, history, or social circumstance." That is more like it. Each and every community is different, with specific issues and unique sets of participants. But each can learn from the lessons of others. What has or has not worked if we try this? Why, or why not? What if we try that instead?

The one universal lesson that can be drawn from the experiences of other communities may be this: with proper planning and consistent execution, localities can attract, retain, and sustain economic growth. And they can derive from it benefits for their constituents while working to minimize the impacts of any unwanted consequences. It requires proper preparation, communitywide involvement, a dedication to the cause, and time. But it can be done.

Notes

1. Porter, *Competitive Strategy,* 11.
2. Ibid., 10.
3. National Governors Association, "The Role of Arts in Economic Development," 8.
4. Hal Cramer, president, Fuels Marketing Division, ExxonMobil, "Thirty Years in Virginia: What We've Learned," presentation to the Virginia Chamber of Commerce, October 29, 2008.

Appendix

Addressing the Critics

In writing this book, and through the course of a career in this field, I have encountered several critical issues about which I feel quite strongly. Curiously, none of the debates over these issues engender clear-cut and obvious solutions. Another way of saying that is this: even the arguments that run counter to my own positions and opinions have merit; even though I may not agree, I certainly see that the counter-arguments bear some logic.

There are numerous areas in which there could be disagreement, but two of these issue areas deserve attention at this point in terms of the positions I have taken and the relevant counterpositions. These issues are the relative merits of growth, tax generation, and sprawl, and the impacts on the quality of life of communities; concerns about the relative pace of economic growth and infrastructure development; and the value and necessity of using economic development incentives.

The question of economic growth and its impacts—both positive and negative—are covered in detail in this book. There are those who will disagree with my position that the generation of tax revenues and the provision of employment opportunities in the community are so critical and provide the resources to pay for schools and other public services that it may be necessary to accept certain levels of unwanted consequences. The argument will certainly be made by some that the resulting sprawl and concerns over environmental impacts are of greater importance than what will be characterized as short-term and short-sided. This is the nature of many no-growth statements.

On the surface, the objectives of no-growth or slow-growth advocates are entirely reasonable. They wish to prevent overcrowding and the loss of a certain quality of life and to preserve open space and the natural surroundings of their communities. Who can argue with that?

Unfortunately, these choices are seldom as black and white as that. A community that doesn't grow can stagnate. It can lose jobs and see its local economy atrophy. It is a fine balancing act to create or attract growth while retaining the original character of the community and the countryside. Because a certain amount of growth is vital to support the provision of public services while minimizing the tax burden on residents, true no-growth is seldom a really feasible strategy. Controlled growth, planned growth, or balanced growth may be monikers that are more indicative of a middle ground in which a community can pursue the positive outcomes of growth while managing the unwanted outcomes.

As with many things, the decisions about where that middle ground lies and how to get there tend to end up being compromises made by communities and their elected leaders. And in the true nature of politics, these decisions are made in the face of a range of competing considerations. It is, however, safe to say that the middle ground seems to shift its location as the larger economy grows and declines. What is acceptable to the majority today may not be tomorrow. Put another way, as the unemployment rate rises, local tolerance for disruption, congestion, and environmental impacts tends to grow.

A related concern in communities where the economy is growing relates to the problems that occur when the pace of development outstrips the existing infrastructure. Growth can be seen as a positive or even a necessary thing, but problems arise when the infrastructure is unable to keep pace. Roads become congested, the supplies of fiber-optic networks and utilities are inadequate, and the community's institutions may not be sufficient to accommodate the growing demand. Increases in the tax base may be sufficient only to accommodate incremental change, leading directly to calls for a moratorium on growth.

Quite often, the timing of the sequence makes it difficult to forestall additional growth even if that is wanted. Once there is a need for additional tax revenues and infrastructure, the one best way to obtain them is to cause the economy to grow. Ultimately, the best that a community can do is to hope to plan well for the growth and to make the best efforts to capitalize on the positive benefits of local economic growth while trying to minimize any unwanted consequences.

The use of economic development incentives to attract or retain businesses is another area that fosters great debate and disagreement. Again, the arguments on both sides of the issue contain reason and logic. Those who oppose the use of incentives do so for the reasons stated earlier in the book. These include concerns about the actual value of projects relative to the incentives offered as well as how to respond to other companies wanting incentives. As well, some will maintain that the use of incentives, if practiced by many competing jurisdictions, will only drive up the price of attracting and retaining businesses in a community. These are all reasonable concerns.

Those who support the use of incentives argue that their community must engage in the practice because so many others do so, and not to do so would place that community at a competitive disadvantage. There is also considerable logic to this perspective. In fact, it is clearly an issue for which there is no comprehensive answer. The fact is that some communities are blessed with the assets that businesses require and others are not. Incentives enable the "have not" communities to compete with the "have" communities. In effect, they are saying to business prospects, "we don't have one or two of the assets you require," or "our competitor may be more attractive to you as a location," "but we are willing to offer you the following things to incentivize you to locate here anyway."

I believe that, in a given situation, either of these arguments can be seen as sensible. Obviously, there is no way to regulate the circumstances under which a state or locality is permitted to engage in the practice of incentives. Therefore, the incentives issue is one about which there may simply have to remain reasonable disagreement.

It strikes me that the debates on these and other issues related to local economic growth need to be less national in nature and more confined to the individual circumstances of localities, regions, and possibly states. What makes sense in one state or region may not make sense elsewhere. Certainly, what makes sense in an urban setting is unlikely to make sense in a rural or even suburban setting. And what makes sense in one community at one point in time may not make sense in that same community at a later time.

It has become an accepted notion that all politics is local. The corollary should be that all economics is local and very personal. The economic growth that occurs or does not occur within a community outweighs an interest in or concern about larger, macro-economic directions. The latter is valuable because it helps frame the local environment, but not as an end in and of itself.

The economic growth that is of greatest importance to individuals is that which takes place on their own Main Street.

Many of these debates and arguments are discussed in this book. To help the reader, I am providing an overview of some of the most salient arguments, and where their debate is discussed in the book. Some occur in multiple sections of the book, as is shown by the page numbers given.

	Argument	*Counterargument*	*Page Numbers*
1	Growth has negative consequences that must be accepted.	Growth yields unacceptable levels of damage to the local quality of life.	47–51, 53–56, 58–59, 85–105
	Also, declining economies result in brain drains, rising crime, and fewer public services.	The negatives may outweigh the positive aspects of growth.	Chapters 6–10
2	Diversification of the local industry base is vital to a sustainable economy.	Not every community can accomplish this.	14–16, Chapter 4

3	Economic growth can be achieved by all communities concurrently.	Economic growth represents a zero-sum game in which one community's gain means another's loss.	13–14, 38–39
4	Communities either grow or die.	A community can remain more or less static over time.	22–23
5	Economic development incentive programs are fraught with problems for communities.	Communities are often forced into providing incentives to be competitive.	32–35
6	In many cases, economic growth is local in nature, rather than regional.	Intraregional competition for economic growth is inefficient.	105–108

Bibliography

Books

Bartik, Timothy J. 1991. *Who Benefits from State and Local Economic Development Policies?* Kalamazoo, Michigan: W.E. Upjohn Institute.

Bernard, Richard M. and Bradley R. Rice. 1983. *Sunbelt Cities: Politics and Growth Since World War II*. Austin, Texas: University of Texas Press.

Bingham, Richard D. and Robert Mier. 1993. *Theories of Local Economic Development: Perspectives from across the Disciplines*. Newbury Park, California: Sage Publishers.

Bruegmann, Robert. 2005. *Sprawl: A Compact History*. Chicago: The University of Chicago Press.

Brunori, David. 2008. *Local Tax Policy: A Federalist Perspective*. Washington, D.C.: The Urban Institute Press.

Downs, Anthony. 1994. *New Visions for Metropolitan America*. Washington, D.C.: Brookings.

Flint, Anthony. 2006. *This Land: The Battle Over Sprawl and the Future of America*. Baltimore: The Johns Hopkins University Press.

Florida, Richard. 2004. *The Rise of the Creative Class and How It Is Transforming Work, Leisure, Community, and Everyday Life*. New York: Basic Books.

Fosler, R. Scott. 1991. *Local Economic Development Strategies for a Changing Economy*. Washington, D.C.: International City Management Association.

Friedman, Benjamin M. 2005. *The Moral Consequences of Economic Growth*. New York: Vintage Books.

Garreau, Joel. 1998. *Edge City: Life on the New Frontier*. New York: Doubleday.

Gillham, Oliver. 2002. *The Limitless City: A Primer on the Urban Sprawl Debate*. Washington, D.C.: Island Press.

Gonzales, Evelyn. 2003. *The Bronx*. New York: Columbia University Press.

Gordon, Gerald L. 1993. *Strategic Planning for Local Government*. Washington, D.C.: International City Management Association.

Henton, Douglas. 1994. *Grass Roots Leaders for a New Economy: How Civic Entrepreneurs are Building Prosperous Economies*. San Francisco: Jossey-Bass.

Hudnut, William H. III. 1998. *Cities on the Rebound: A Vision for Urban America*. Washington, D.C.: The Urban Institute.

Jacobs, Jane. 1992. *The Death and Life of Great American Cities*. New York: Random House.

Kanter, Rosabeth Moss. 1997. *World Class: Thriving in the Global Economy*. New York: Touchstone.

Kotkin, Joel. 2000. *The New Geography: How the Digital Revolution Is Reshaping the American Landscape*. New York: Random House.

Lubove, Roy. 1996. *Twentieth Century Pittsburgh: Government, Business, and Environmental Change*. Pittsburgh: University of Pittsburgh Press.

———. 2004. *Twentieth Century Pittsburgh: The Post-Steel Era*. Pittsburgh: University of Pittsburgh Press.

Lynch, Robert G. 2004. *Rethinking Growth Strategies: How State and Local Taxes and Services Affect Economic Development*. Washington, D.C.: Economic Policy Institute.

———. 2007. *Arts and Economic Prosperity*. Washington, D.C.: Americans for the Arts.

Madrick, Jeff. 2002. *Why Economies Grow: The Forces That Shape Prosperity and How We Can Get Them Working Again*. New York: Basic Books.

Marshall, Alex. 2005. *How Cities Work: Suburbs, Sprawl, and the Roads Not Taken*. Austin: University of Texas Press.

Mills, Edwin S. and John F. McDonald. 1992. *Sources of Metropolitan Growth*. New Brunswick, New Jersey: Center for Urban Policy Research.

O'Sullivan, Arthur. 2007. *Urban Economics*. New York: McGraw-Hill/Irwin.

O'Toole, Randall. 2001. *The Vanishing Automobile and Other Urban Myths: How Smart Growth Will Harm American Cities*. Bandon, Oregon: The Thoreau Institute.

Pack, Jane Rothenberg. 2002. *Growth and Convergence in Metropolitan America*. Washington, D.C.: Brookings Institution.

Porter, Michael E. 1980. *Competitive Strategy*. New York: The Free Press.

Sarzyonski, Andre, Marilyn A. Brown, and Frank Southworth. 2008. *Shrinking the Global Footprint of Metropolitan America*. Washington, D.C.: The Brookings Institution.

Shaffer, Ron. 2004. *Community Economics: Linking Theory and Practice*. Ames, Iowa: The University of Iowa Press.

Stimson, Roger J., Roger Stough, and Brian Roberts. 2006. *Regional Economic Development: Analysis and Planning Strategy*. New York: Springer.

Vaughn, Robert. 1986. *Financing Economic Development in the South: Public Infrastructure and Entrepreneurship*. Washington, D.C.: Commission on the Future of the South, Southern Growth Policies Board.

Weinstein, Bernard L. 1985. *Regional Growth and Decline in the United States*. New York: Praeger.

Journals

Artz, Georgeanne. Fourth Quarter 2003. Rural Area Brain Drain: Is it a Reality? *Choices*.

Bartik, Timothy. December 1994. Jobs, Productivity, and Local Economic Development: What Implications Does Economic Research Have for the Role of Local Government? *National Tax Journal* 47(4): 847–62.

Bean, Frank and Mark A. Leach. 2005. A Critical Disjuncture? The Culmination of Post-World War II Socio-Demographic and Economic Trends in the United States. *Journal of Population Research* 22(1): 63–78.

Blair, Robert. Fall 1998. Strategic Planning for Economic Development: A Suggested Model for Program Evaluation. *Public Administration Quarterly* 22(3): 331–48.

Bowman, Ann O. 1988. Competition for Economic Development among Southeastern Cities. *Urban Affairs Quarterly* 23(4): 511–27.

Bradbury, Katherine L., Yolanda K. Kodrzycki, and Robert Tannenwald. March–April 1997. The Effects of State and Local Public Policies on Economic Development: An Overview. *New England Economic Journal:* 1–13.

Burns, Katie. July 6, 2004. In the Country or City, Boosting Local Economic Development Remains a Challenge. *Economic Development Now* 4(13).

"Challenges and Opportunities Ahead," Chicago: Federal Reserve Bank, 1996.

Cisneros, Henry. September 1995. Urban Entrepreneurialism and National Economic Growth, *Cityscape:* 55–70.

Dietrick, Sabina and Cliff Ellis. Autumn 2004. New Urbanism in the Inner City: A Case Study of Pittsburgh. *Journal of the American Planning Association* 70(4): 426–42.

Elkins, David R. and Elaine B. Sharp. 2000. Neighborhood Challenges to Economic Development. *International Journal of Public Administration* 23(9): 1651–78.

Evans, Mel and Stephen Syrett. Fall 1998. Generating Social Capital: The Social Economy and Local Economic Development. *European Urban and Regional Studies* 14(1): 55–74.

Feiock, Richard C. 2000. Regulatory Reform, Property Rights, and Economic Development. *International Journal of Public Administration* 23(9): 1599–1620.

Feiock, Richard C. and Christopher Stream. 2001. Environmental Protection and Economic Development: A False Trade-Off? *Public Administration Review* 61(3): 313–21.

Hall, Jeremy L. January/February 2008. The Forgotten Regional Organizations: Creating Capacity for Economic Development. *Public Administration Review* 68(1): 24–35.

———. 2007. Understanding State Economic Development Policy in the New Economy: A Theoretical Foundation and Empirical Examination of State Innovation in the United States. *Public Administration Review* 67(4): 630–45.

Harris, Richard and Robert Lewis. March 2001. The Geography of North American Cities and Suburbs: 1900–1950. *Journal of Urban History* 27(3): 259–62.

Henry, Mark and Mark Drabenscott. Second Quarter 1996. A New Micro View of the U.S. Rural Economy. *Economic Review* (Federal Reserve Bank of Kansas City) 53–70.

Howell-Moroney, Michael. Spring 2005. Economic Implementation Constraints on Preserving Land from Sprawl: The Case of the Delaware Valley. *Public Administration Quarterly* 29(1): 55–77.

James, Franklin J. June 1995. Urban Economies: Trends, Forces, and Implications for the President's National Urban Policy. *Cityscape* 1(2): 67–123.

Jones, Bryan D. and Arnold Vedlitz. 1988. Higher Education Policies and Economic Growth in the American States. *Economic Development Quarterly* 2(1): 78–87.

Kanhon, Kan. November 2002. Residential Mobility with Job Location Uncertainty. *Journal of Urban Economics* 52(3): 501–23.

Knack, Stephen and Phillip Keefer. 1997. Does Social Capital Have and Economic Payoff: A Cross-Country Investigation. *Quarterly Journal of Economics* 112(4): 1251–88.

Kuotsai, Tom L. 2001. Governance and Economic Development: Changes and Challenges. *International Journal of Public Administration* 24(10): 1005–22.

Landis, John. Autumn 2006. Growth Management Revisited: Efficiency, Price Effects, and Displacement. *Journal of the American Planning Association* 72(4): 411–30.

Lejano, Raul and Anne Wessels. August 2006. Community and Economic Development: Seeking Common Ground in Discourse and in Practice. *Urban Studies* 43(9): 1469–89.

Lopez, Russ and Patricia Hynes. January 2003. Sprawl in the 1990's: Measurement, Distribution, and Trends. *Urban Affairs Review* 38(3): 325–55.

Markley, Deborah M. Winter 2006. A Framework for Developing Rural Entrepreneurship. *Economic Development America* 4–6.

McGuire, Michael et al. 1994. Building Development Capacity in Nonmetropolitan Communities. *Public Administration Review* 54(5): 426–33.

Olberding, Julie C. July/August 2002. Does Regionalism Beget Regionalism?: The Relationship Between Norms and Regional Partnerships for Economic Development. *Public Administration Review* 62(4): 480–91.

Peters, Alan and Peter Fisher. Winter 2004. The Failures of Economic Development Incentives. *Journal of the American Planning Association* 70(1): 27–37.

Plosila, Walter. Winter 2005. Building Innovation-Driven Regional Economies in Small and Mid-Sized Metro Centers. *Economic Development America* 4–7.

Polese, Mario. July 2005. Cities and National Economic Growth: A Reappraisal. *Urban Studies* 42(8): 1429–51.

Poole, Kenneth E. et al. August 1999. Evaluating Business Development Incentives. *Economic Development America*.

Porter, Michael E. November–December 1998. Clusters and the New Economics of Competition, *Harvard Business Review:* 77–90.

———. December 2005. Clusters of Innovation: Regional Foundations of U.S. Competitiveness. *On the Frontier.*

———. 2000. Location, Competition, and Economic Development: Local Clusters in a Global Economy. *Economic Development Quarterly* 14(1): 15–34.

———. May-June 1995. The Competitive Advantage of the Inner City." *Harvard Business Review:* 55–71.

Raco, Mike. May 1999. Competition, Collaboration, and the New Industrial Districts: Examining the Institutional Turn in Local Economic Development. *Urban Studies* 36(5/6): 951–68.

Reese, Laura A. and Raymond A. Rosenfeld. September 2004. Local Economic Development in the United States and Canada: Institutionalizing Policy Approaches. *American Review of Public Administration* 34(3): 277–92.

———. July 2002. Reconsidering Private Sector Power: Business Input and Local Development Policy. *Urban Affairs Review* 37(1): 642–74.

Richmond, Karin. Fall 2006. Clawbacks in Economic Development: Policies and Practices. *Economic Development America.*

Rubin, Barry M. and C. Kurt Zorn. 1985. Sensible State and Local Economic Development. *Public Administration Review* 45(2): 333–9.

Rypkema, Donovan. Winter 2003. The Importance of Downtown in the 21st Century. *Journal of the American Planning Association* 69(1): 9–15.

Shaffer, Ron. May 1995. Dying Communities. *Community Economics Newsletter.*

Sigelman, Lee and Jeffrey Henig. September 2001. Crossing the Great Divide: Race and Preferences for Living in the City vs. the Suburbs. *Urban Affairs Review* 37(1): 3–18.

Waits, Mary Jo. 2000. Economic Development Strategies in the American States. *International Journal of Public Administration* 23(9): 1541–71.

Wolman, Harold and David Spitzley. 1996. The Politics of Local Economic Development. *Economic Development Quarterly* 10(2): 115–51.

Worden, Michael A. and David A. de Kok. Spring 2002. Population Growth in Arizona

Zovanyi, Gabor. October 1999. The Growth Management Delusion. *NPG Forum.*

Online Sources

"171 Years of Houston History," http://www.houstonhistory.com/decades/history59.htm.

"A Brief History of Silicon Valley," Jim McCormick, http://people.seas.harvard.edu/joues/shockley/siliconvalley.html.

"Arts Essential to Economic Growth," Chris Farrell, Marketplace, http://marketplace.publicradio.org/display/uob/2006/11/16/arts-essential_to_economic_growth.htm, November 16, 2006.

"Census of Housing," Washington, D.C.: U.S. Bureau of the Census, 2004.

"Berkeley Roundtable on the International Economy," Silicon Valley, Berkeley, California, May 1, 1993.

"Biotech, Infotech, Nanotech Poised to Alter 21st Century Economies," Bruce Felps, http://www.masshightech.com/stories/2002/04/29/story81, April 29, 2002.

"Building the Rural Economy with High Growth Entrepreneurs," Jason Henderson, Federal Reserve Bank of Kansas City, http://www.kc.frb.org.

"Clark County and Nevada Populations, 1970–2007," Center for Business and Economic Research, University of Nevada at Las Vegas, http://cber.unlv.edu/pop.html.

"Development without Eminent Domain," Curt Pringle, Perspectives on Eminent Domain Abuse, http://www.castlecoalition.org/pdf/publications/Perspectives-Pringle, June 2007.

"Economic Overview of Metropolitan Las Vegas," The Center for Business and Economic Research, University of Nevada at Las Vegas, http://cber.unlv.edu/stats.html.

"Education as a Rural Development Strategy," Robert Gibbs, Amber Waves, http://www.ers.usda.gov/amber waves/november/05/features/education.htm, November 2005.

"High Technology Clusters in Silicon Valley," American University, Kogod School, Washington, D.C., http://www.american.edu/academic.depts/h-sb/citge/silicon%20valley%202.htm, 2002.

"Hill Briefing on Social and Economic Consequences of Job Loss Draws Crowd," Johanna Ebner, http://asanet.org'footnotes'april04/indextwo.html, April 2004.

"Historical Census of Housing Tables," http://www.census.gov/uues/www/housing/census/historic/owner.html.

"Historical Economic Data for Metropolitan Las Vegas," http://cber.unlv.edu/snoutlk.html.

"House of Cards—Las Vegas: Too Many People in the Wrong Place, Celebrating as a Way of Life," Mike Davis, Radical Urban Theory, http://www.radicalurbantheory.com/davis/housecards.html.

"Houston Business—A Perspective on the Houston Economy," Federal Reserve Bank of Dallas, http://www.dallas-fed.org/research/houston/2000/hb0006.html, September 2000.

"Justices Affirm Property Seizures," Charles Lamb, WashingtonPost.com, http://www.washingtonpost.com/wp-dyn/content/article/2005/06/23/AR, June 24, 2005.

"Local Economic Development for the 1990s," U.S. Department of Housing and Urban Development, http://www.hud.user.org?periodicals/rrr/econdev.html.

"Maine Passes Law Requiring Economic Impact Studies of Big Box Projects," The Hometown Advantage, http://www.newrules.org/retail/news, June 18, 2007.

"More Jobs?: No Thank You, Say Oregon's Mandarins," Andrew Cave, http://www.telegraph.co.uk/html.content.jhtml?html=/archive/1999/06/10/cuore10.html, June 1, 1999.

"Our Legacy: Oil Glut and the Economic Downturn," http://www.houstonhistory.com/legacy/history6t.htm, 2008.

"Outcome of Portland Experiment Still Uncertain," http://www.sprawlcity.org/portland.html.

"Population of the 100 Largest Urban Places," U.S. Bureau of the Census Reports, http://www.census.gov/population/www/documentation/twps0027/tab20.txt.

"Portland: Urban Growth Boundary Keeps Out Growth," Demographia, http://www.demographia.com/db-pougbmivg.pdf.

"Power at the Local Level: Growth Coalition Theory," G. William Domhoff, Who Rules America? http://sociology.ucsc.edu/whorulesamerica/power/local.html, November 2007.

"Puget Sound Trends," Puget Sound Regional Council, http://www.info@psrc.org, November 2007.

"Regional Economic Profiles. Report Series of Bureau of Economic Affairs," http://www.bea.gov/bea/regional/reis/action.cfm.

"Rosie the Riveter: Women Working during World War II," http://www.ups.gov/pwro/collection/website/rosie.htm.

"Rural Economic Development: What Makes Rural Communities Grow?" Lorna Aldrich and Lorin Kusmin, http://usda.gov/ruraleconomicdevelopment.html, September 1992.

"Rust Belt," Answers.com, http://www.answers.com/topic/rust-belt.

"Santa Clara County: California's Silicon Valley," http://www.ups.gov/history/nr/travel/santaclara/economic.htm.

"Seattle Economic Trends," American Life, Inc., http://www.amlife.us/economic_trends.html.

"Stephen's Web," Silicon Valley, http://www.downes.ca/cgi-bin/page.cgi?topic=164."The Taking of Property: *Kelo v. New London* and the Economics of Eminent Domain," Thomas A. Garrett and Paul Rothstein, Federal Reserve Reports, http://www.stlouisfed.org/publications/ne/2007/a/pages/prosperity.html, 2007.

"The Austin/San Antonio Corridor: The Dynamics of a Developing Technopolis," Raymond W. Smilor, George Kozmetsky, and David V. Gibson, http://www.utexas.edu/depts/ic2/pubs/corr, 1987.

"The Creative Class: A Key to Rural Growth," David A. McGranahan and Timothy R. Wojan, Amber Waves, http://www.iers.usda.gov/amberwaves/april07/features/creative.htm, April 2007.

"The Growth Management Delusion," http://www.npg.org/forum_series/growthmgmt_delusion.htm, October 1999.

"The History of Las Vegas," Aaron Walburg, http://www.ucgc.org/2002/07-26_las_vegas/history.htm, June 26, 1992.

"The Post-War Economy: 1945–1960. http://economics.about.com/od/useconomichistory/a/post_war.htm.

"Urban Growth Boundary. http://www.metro-region.org/index.cfm/go/by.web/id/277.

"What Is Smart Growth?" Westmoreland County, http://www.smartgrowth.org/whatis.asp (accessed September 7, 2008).

"Women in World War II," http://netfiles.uiuc.edu/xtang2/www/w3.html.

Presentations

Cramer, Hal, president, Fuels Marketing, ExxonMobil. October 21, 2008. "Thirty Years in Virginia: What We've Learned." A presentation to the Virginia Economic Summit of the Virginia Chamber of Commerce.

Florida, Richard. 2007. "The Creative Economy." Presentation to the National Conference on the Creative Economy, Fairfax, Virginia.

Ketels, Christian H. M. May 9, 2003. "Cluster-Based Economic Development." Presentation to the Economic Development Administration Annual Conference, Washington, D.C.
————. December 5, 2003. "The Development of the Cluster Concept—Present Experiences and Further Development." Prepared for NRW Conference on Clusters, Duisburg, Germany.
Loveridge, Scott. April 2000. "A Behavioral Approach to Understanding Local Leader Incentives in Economic Development." Presented to the Southern Regional Science Association annual meeting, Miami Beach, Florida.
Moskow, Michael. February 6, 2007. "Challenges and Opportunities Ahead." University of Chicago.
Olson, Mark W. July 26, 2002. "Economic Change in Rural America." Remarks to the Fergus Falls Rotary Club, Fergus Falls, Minnesota.
Pollack, Elliott D. "How We Got Here—A Triumph of Will: An Economic History of Greater Phoenix." A Presentation to the Arizona Historical Foundation. February 23, 2005.

Unpublished Papers

Atkinson, Robert D. "Reversing Rural America's Economic Decline." *Progressive.* February 2004.
Atkinson, Robert D. and Scott Andes. "The 2008 State New Economy Index." Kauffman Foundation and the Information Technology and Innovation Foundation: Washington, D.C., 2008.
Barkley, David L. "Employment Generation Strategies for Small Towns: An Overview of Alternatives." September 2001.
Bartik, Timothy. "Economic Development Strategies." W.E. UpJohn Institute: Kalamazoo, Michigan, January 1995.
Bates, Timothy. "Alleviating the Lagging Performance of Economically Depressed Communities and Regions." Published by Commonwealth Institute, Cambridge, Massachusetts.
Breslow, Marc. "Economic Development Subsidies in Maine: Modest Job Gains at High Cost." December 15, 1999.
Brouder, Ann-Marie and Lorna Berry. "Sustainable Business Clusters in the Regions," *The Regional Futures Report.* February 2004.
Bureau of Labor Statistics. "Occupational Outlook: 2008-2009. "Washington, D.C.: United States Department of Labor. 2007.
Cohen, Stephen S. and Clara Eugenia Garcia. "Learning from California: The Macroeconomic Consequences of Structural Changes."
Cortright, Joseph. "New Growth Theory, Technology and Learning: A Practitioner Guide." Economic Development Administration. 2001.
Cortright, Joseph and Heike Mayer. "Spinoffs, Startups, and Fast Growth Firms in the Portland Regional Economy." February 2000.
Dardia et al. "Defense Cutbacks: Effects on California Communities, Firms, and Workers." 1995. Santa Monica, California: The Rand Corporation.
"Economic Analysis of the Central Puget Sound Region." September 27, 2005. Prepared for the Puget Sound Regional Council, Seattle.
"Economic Base Theory." Florida State University.
"Eminent Domain Resource Kit." International Economic Development Council.

Finkle, Jeffrey A. "Location Incentives are Unfair and Poorly Justified." International Economic Development Council.

Fruth, William. "The Flow of Money and its Impact on Local Economies." National Association of Industrial and Office Parks.

Hevesi, Alan. "Smart Growth in New York State: A Discussion Paper." Albany: Comptroller's Press Office. May 2004.

Huckell/Weinman Associates, Inc. "Economic Contribution of the Health Care Industry to the City of Seattle." City of Seattle Office of Economic Development. September 2004.

"Incentives: An Economic Development Guide." Washington, D.C.: The International Economic Development Council.

Kingsley, G. Thomas, and Kathryn L.S. Pettit. "Population Growth and Decline in City Neighborhoods." *Change in Urban America*. Washington, D.C.: The Urban Institute. December 18, 2002.

"Lenoir County Economic Development Summit." Kinston, North Carolina: October 1999.

Long Island Association, The. "A Tale of Two Suburbs." *The Long Island Index*. March 2007.

Lowery, Ying. "Dynamics of Minority-Owned Employer Establishments, 1997–2001." *Small Business Research Summary*. Washington, D.C. United States Small Business Administration. February 2005.

Lynch, Robert L. "Arts and Economic Prosperity." Americans for the Arts. 2007.

"Market Street Services, Economic Performance: Austin." Austin, Texas, May 27, 2003.

Mineta, Norman Y. "The Minority Business Challenge.' United States Department of Commerce. September 25, 2000.

Moore, Gordon and Kevin Davis. "Learning the Silicon Valley Way." Stanford, California: Stanford Institute for Economic Policy Research. June 15, 2001.

National Association of State Development Agencies. "Evaluating Business Development Incentives." Washington, D.C., August 1999.

National Governors Association. "The Role of Arts in Economic Development." Washington, D.C., June 25, 2001.

Osborne, Tom. "Revitalizing Rural Nebraska." Rural Economic Development Handbook and Resource Guide. 2004.

Perryman Group. "Paths to Prosperity: Strategic Job Growth Parameters for Opportunity Houston through 2005." Waco, Texas. May 2006.

"Public Sector Economic Development: Concepts and Approaches for Local, Regional, and State Action." Northeast-Midwest Institute.

Puget Sound Regional Council. "Development Patterns Shift under Growth Management." Seattle: PSRC. April 2008.

———. "Populations of Cities and Towns." Seattle: PSRC. September 2007.

———. "Puget Sound Trends: Recession and Rebound in Target Industry Groups, 2000–2006." Seattle: PSRC. November 2007.

Redman, Andy. 'Another Tale of Two Cities." Austin, Texas: Ray Marshall Center for the Study of Human Resources. May 2004.

Robinson, Ryan. "Austin Area Population Histories and Forecasts." Austin: Department of Planning. January 2008.

Shear, Emmett. "Seattle: Boom and Busts." New London, Connecticut: Yale University. 2002.

Sims, Richard G. "School Funding, Taxes, and Economic Growth." Chicago: The Federal Reserve Bank. April 2004.

Statistical Abstract of the United States, Washington, D.C.: United States Bureau of the Census, 2003.

Treado, Carey and Frank Giarratani. "Intermediate Steel Industry Suppliers in the Pittsburgh Region: A Cluster-Based Analysis of Regional Economic Resilience." Pittsburgh: Center for Industry Studies, University of Pittsburgh. December 2008.

U.S. Bureau of the Census. "Sprawl City: Outcome of Portland's Experiment Still Uncertain." Washington, D.C.: Department of Commerce. 2007.

Vedder, Richard. "State and Local Taxes and Economic Growth." *Virginia Viewpoint.* November 2003.

Wells, Barbara. "Smart Growth at the Frontier: Strategies and Resources for Rural Communities." Northeast-Midwest Institute.

Interviews

Adams, Scott, director, and Betea, Romeo, deputy director, Las Vegas (Nevada) Economic Development Office, interviewed by Gerald L. Gordon, August 11, 2008.

Hamilton, Brian, Austin (Texas) Office of Economic Development, interviewed by Gerald L. Gordon, August 7, 2008.

Knutson, Deborah, director, Snohomish County (Washington) Economic Development Council, interviewed by Gerald L. Gordon, October 2008.

Priest, Tim, CEO, Greenlight Greater Portland, interviewed by Gerald L. Gordon, October 3, 2008.

Richard, Craig J., senior vice president, Opportunity Houston, interviewed by Gerald L. Gordon, October 20, 2008.

Index